William Shakespeare's

Hamlet

In Plain and Simple English

A SwipeSpeare™ Book
www.SwipeSpeare.com

Table of Contents

About This Series 3

Characters 4

    Act I...**5**

      Scene I 6

      Scene II 12

      Scene III 20

      Scene IV 24

      SCENE V 27

    Act II **33**

      Scene I 34

      Scene II 38

    Act III...**55**

      Scene I 56

      Scene II 62

      Scene III...75

      Scene IV 78

    Act IV **85**

      Scene I 86

      Scene II 88

      Scene III 90

      Scene IV 93

      Scene V 95

      Scene VI 102

      Scene VII 103

    Act V **109**

      Scene I 110

      Scene II 120

About This Series

The "SwipeSpeare™" series started as a way of telling Shakespeare for the modern reader—being careful to preserve the themes and integrity of the original. Visit our website SwipeSpeare.com to see other books in the series, as well as the interactive, and swipe-able, app!

The series is expanding every month. Visit BookCaps.com to see non-Shakespeare books in this series, and while you are there join the Facebook page, so you are first to know when a new book comes out.

Context about the company which helped with the translation of the piece

Characters

Claudius, King of Denmark.

Hamlet, Son to the former, and Nephew to the present King.

Polonius, Lord Chamberlain.

Horatio, Friend to Hamlet.

Laertes, Son to Polonius.

Voltimand, Courtier.

Cornelius, Courtier.

Rosencrantz, Courtier.

Guildenstern, Courtier.

Osric, Courtier.

A Gentleman, Courtier.

A Priest.

Marcellus, Officer.

Bernardo, Officer.

Francisco, a Soldier

Reynaldo, Servant to Polonius.

Players.

Two Clowns, Grave-diggers.

Fortinbras, Prince of Norway.

A Captain.

English Ambassadors.

Ghost of Hamlet's Father.

Gertrude, Queen of Denmark, and Mother of Hamlet.

Ophelia, Daughter to Polonius.

Lords, Ladies, Officers, Soldiers, Sailors, Messengers, and other

Attendants.

[handwritten note: Usually characters are listed by importance, is Claudius more significant in Hamlet than Hamlet is?]

Act I

I am excited to read this story and compare
and contrast it to the film watched over the
summer.

Scene I

Elsinore. A platform before the castle

FRANCISCO at his post. Enter to him BERNARDO

BERNARDO
Who's there?

Who's there?

FRANCISCO
Nay, answer me: stand, and unfold yourself.

No, you answer me. Identify yourself.

BERNARDO
Long live the king!

I am an officer in the king's court.

[handwritten: Both suspicious of who the other is]

FRANCISCO
Bernardo?

BERNARDO
He.

Yes.

FRANCISCO
You come most carefully upon your hour.

You are late.

BERNARDO
'Tis now struck twelve; get thee to bed, Francisco.

It's only twelve o' clock. Go to bed already, Francisco.

FRANCISCO
For this relief much thanks: 'tis bitter cold,
And I am sick at heart.

Thanks. It's cold and I am sick of it.

BERNARDO
Have you had quiet guard?

Have things been quiet on your guard?

[handwritten: no criminal acts in / around the castle]

FRANCISCO
Not a mouse stirring.

Quiet as a mouse.

BERNARDO
Well, good night.
If you do meet Horatio and Marcellus,
The rivals of my watch, bid them make haste.

Well, good night.
If you see Horatio and Marcellus,
tell them to hurry up.

FRANCISCO
I think I hear them. Stand, ho! Who's there?

I think I hear them now. Stop! Who's there?

[handwritten: quick intro to 2 new characters]

Enter HORATIO and MARCELLUS

HORATIO
Friends to this ground.

We are friends.

MARCELLUS
And liegemen to the Dane.

And we work for the Dane.

FRANCISCO
Give you good night.

Be on your way then.

MARCELLUS
O, farewell, honest soldier:

Goodbye, soldier.

Who hath relieved you?

[handwritten: they are switching out who is being on warm]

FRANCISCO
Bernardo has my place. →
Give you good night.

Who has relieved you?

Bernardo took my place.
Good night.

Exit

MARCELLUS
Holla! Bernardo!

[handwritten: Interesting to address himself in the third person]

Hey! Bernardo!

BERNARDO
Say,
What, is Horatio there?

What?
Is that you, Horatio?

HORATIO
A piece of him. →

A part of me is here.

BERNARDO
Welcome, Horatio: welcome, good Marcellus.

Welcome, Horatio and Marcellus.

MARCELLUS
What, has this thing appear'd again to-night?

Has that thing appeared again tonight?

BERNARDO
I have seen nothing.

[handwritten: → What did Marcellus see?]

I haven't seen anything.

MARCELLUS
he will see for himself.
Horatio says 'tis but our fantasy,
And will not let belief take hold of him
Touching this dreaded sight, twice seen of us:
Therefore I have entreated him along
With us to watch the minutes of this night;
That if again this apparition come,
He may approve our eyes and speak to it.

Horatio doesn't believe me;
says it is all in my head.
We have seen the ghost twice.
so I invited him to
stand guard with us tonight.
If the apparition comes,
he will see for himself.

HORATIO
Tush, tush, 'twill not appear.

Nonsense. It will not appear again.

BERNARDO

Sit down awhile;
And let us once again assail your ears,
That are so fortified against our story
What we have two nights seen. →

[handwritten: claims to have seen ghosts]

Let's sit down
and we will tell you,
although you are skeptical,
what we have seen the last two nights.

HORATIO
Well, sit we down,
And let us hear Bernardo speak of this.

Ok, let's sit.
I will listen to Bernardo's story.

BERNARDO
Last night of all,
When yond same star that's westward from the pole
Had made his course to illume that part of heaven
Where now it burns, Marcellus and myself,
The bell then beating one,--

Last night,
about one o'clock, with the light from that star in the west,
Marcellus and I—

Enter Ghost

[handwritten: Interesting part to have to play]

MARCELLUS
Peace, break thee off; look, where it comes again!

Be quiet. Look, here it comes again!

BERNARDO
In the same figure, like the king that's dead.

It looks just like the dead king.

[handwritten: does not seem affected by the ghost]

MARCELLUS
Thou art a scholar; speak to it, Horatio.

You are smart, Horatio, speak to it.

BERNARDO
Looks it not like the king? mark it, Horatio.

It does look like the king; doesn't it, Horatio?

HORATIO
Most like: it harrows me with fear and wonder.

It does, and I'm both scared and curious.

[handwritten: he is both scared and curious]

BERNARDO
It would be spoke to.

It acts like it wants to say something.

MARCELLUS
Question it, Horatio.

Ask it something, Horatio.

HORATIO
What art thou that usurp'st this time of night,
Together with that fair and warlike form
In which the majesty of buried Denmark
Did sometimes march? by heaven I charge thee, speak!

What are you out at the time of night
ready for war and resembling
the dead king of Denmark?
In the name of God, say something!

MARCELLUS
It is offended.

It is offended.

BERNARDO
See, it stalks away!

See, it's going away!

HORATIO
Stay! speak, speak! I charge thee, speak!

Wait, stay. Speak! I command you to speak!

[handwritten: What was the significance of that?]

Exit Ghost

MARCELLUS
'Tis gone, and will not answer.

It's gone and would not say anything.

BERNARDO
How now, Horatio!
you tremble and look pale:
Is not this something more than fantasy?
What think you on't?

What do you think now,
Horatio? You look a little pale and scared.
You think it's more than some fantasy?

[handwritten: Calling him out for not believing]

HORATIO
Before my God, I might not this believe
Without the sensible and true avouch
Of mine own eyes.

I swear, I never would have believed
if I hadn't seen it
with my own eyes.

MARCELLUS
Is it not like the king?

Doesn't it look like the king?

HORATIO
As thou art to thyself:
Such was the very armour he had on
When he the ambitious Norway combated;
So frown'd he once, when, in an angry parle,
He smote the sledded Polacks on the ice.

I know that armor as well as I know myself.
He wore it during the battle with Norway
when he killed the Polacks on their sleds.
So strange.

[handwritten: looks like a dead king]

'Tis strange.

→ Interesting to note that it was at the same time

MARCELLUS
Thus twice before, and jump at this dead hour,
With martial stalk hath he gone by our watch.

*This is the second time at this very hour
that it has walked around like a soldier.*

HORATIO
In what particular thought to work I know not;
But in the gross and scope of my opinion,
This bodes some strange eruption to our state. *↝*

*I don't know what this means,
but I have a funny feeling something
is going to happen in our country.*

Bad omen/ foreshadowing

MARCELLUS
Good now, sit down, and tell me, he that knows,
Why this same strict and most observant watch
So nightly toils the subject of the land,
And why such daily cast of brazen cannon,
And foreign mart for implements of war;
Why such impress of shipwrights, whose sore task
Does not divide the Sunday from the week;
What might be toward, that this sweaty haste
Doth make the night joint-labourer with the day:
Who is't that can inform me?

*Okay, let's sit down and talk about what is going on.
Why do we stand guard every night, and why
are cannons being made?
Why are we buying foreign weapons and ships
are being built every day of the week.
Do you think something is about to happen?*

HORATIO
That can I;
At least, the whisper goes so. Our last king,
Whose image even but now appear'd to us,
Was, as you know, by Fortinbras of Norway,
Thereto prick'd on by a most emulate pride,
Dared to the combat; in which our valiant Hamlet--
For so this side of our known world esteem'd him--
Did slay this Fortinbras; who by a seal'd compact,
Well ratified by law and heraldry,
Did forfeit, with his life, all those his lands
Which he stood seized of, to the conqueror:
Against the which, a moiety competent
Was gaged by our king; which had return'd
To the inheritance of Fortinbras,
Had he been vanquisher; as, by the same covenant,
And carriage of the article design'd,
His fell to Hamlet. Now, sir, young Fortinbras,
Of unimproved mettle hot and full,
Hath in the skirts of Norway here and there
Shark'd up a list of lawless resolutes,
For food and diet, to some enterprise
That hath a stomach in't; which is no other--
As it doth well appear unto our state--
But to recover of us, by strong hand
And terms compulsatory, those foresaid lands
So by his father lost: and this, I take it, ──→
Is the main motive of our preparations,
The source of this our watch and the chief head
Of this post-haste and romage in the land.

↑ Hamlet killed the king that they just saw

revenge is a powerful motive

*I think I know.
As you know, the king, we just saw in his ghostly form,
was the enemy of Fortinbras, the king of Norway.
Fortinbras dared the king to fight and was killed
by the seemingly valiant Hamlet.
According to a signed contract, Fortinbras forfeited his land,
as well as his life, to his conqueror.
Our king had signed a similar contract.
Now, his son, the young Fortinbras, seeks revenge
and the return of his father's land.
He has commissioned the help of some lawless men.
I think that is the reason for the frenzy of activity,
including our watch and the procurement of weapons.*

BERNARDO
I think it be no other but e'en so:
Well may it sort that this portentous figure
Comes armed through our watch; so like the king
That was and is the question of these wars,

*I think you're right.
That explains why the king, responsible for these wars,
comes walking around in his armor on our watch.*

HORATIO

A mote it is to trouble the mind's eye.
(The cock crows.) Stay and speak! Stop the ghost, Marcellus.

In the most high and palmy state of Rome,
A little ere the mightiest Julius fell, → *Allusion to Julius Caesar*
The graves stood tenantless and the sheeted dead
Did squeak and gibber in the Roman streets:
As stars with trains of fire and dews of blood,
Disasters in the sun; and the moist star
Upon whose influence Neptune's empire stands
Was sick almost to doomsday with eclipse:
And even the like precurse of fierce events,
As harbingers preceding still the fates
And prologue to the omen coming on,
Have heaven and earth together demonstrated
Unto our climatures and countrymen.--
But soft, behold! lo, where it comes again!
Re-enter Ghost → *He is back again!*
I'll cross it, though it blast me. Stay, illusion!
If thou hast any sound, or use of voice,
Speak to me:
If there be any good thing to be done,
That may to thee do ease and grace to me,
Speak to me:
Cock crows
If thou art privy to thy country's fate,
Which, happily, foreknowing may avoid, O, speak!
Or if thou hast uphoarded in thy life
Extorted treasure in the womb of earth,
For which, they say, you spirits oft walk in death,
Speak of it: stay, and speak! Stop it, Marcellus. → *how does one Stop a ghost?*

There is definitely trouble brewing.

Even in the great city of Rome,
before the murder of Julius Caesar,
the dead arose from their graves
and walked the streets, speaking gibberish.
There were other signs and omens, too,
like shooting stars and solar eclipses.
The fates are warning us. But wait!
Here comes the ghost again! (Enter Ghost.)
I'll go to it, even though I don't want to. Stay, ghost.
If you can, speak to me. If there is anything I can do
to ease your pain, tell me. Or, if you know something
that would help our country, please speak.
If you have some hidden treasure here on earth,
which makes you uneasy, let us help you.
(The cock crows.) Stay and speak! Stop the ghost, Marcellus.

MARCELLUS

Shall I strike at it with my partisan?

Should I hit it with my sword?

HORATIO

Do, if it will not stand.

Yes, if it doesn't stop.

BERNARDO

'Tis here!

It's here!

HORATIO

'Tis here!

It's here!

MARCELLUS *Such a strange character*

'Tis gone!
Exit Ghost
We do it wrong, being so majestical,
To offer it the show of violence;
For it is, as the air, invulnerable,
And our vain blows malicious mockery. *Must honor the king - ghost*

It's gone!
(Exit Ghost.)
We shouldn't have used force on the ghost of the king.
Anyway, it is an apparition and can't be touched.
We were stupid to think otherwise.

BERNARDO

It was about to speak, when the cock crew.

It was about to speak when the cock crowed.

HORATIO

And then it started like a guilty thing
Upon a fearful summons. I have heard,
The cock, that is the trumpet to the morn,

And then it started to act scared like someone guilty of a crime.
I have heard when the cock crows, a sign that day is
approaching, ghosts must return to where their spirits are

Doth with his lofty and shrill-sounding throat
Awake the god of day; and, at his warning,
Whether in sea or fire, in earth or air,
The extravagant and erring spirit his
To his confine: and of the truth herein
This present object made probation.

confined. We just saw that for ourselves.

MARCELLUS
It faded on the crowing of the cock.
Some say that ever 'gainst that season comes
Wherein our Saviour's birth is celebrated,
The bird of dawning singeth all night long:
And then, they say, no spirit dares stir abroad;
The nights are wholesome; then no planets strike,
No fairy takes, nor witch hath power to charm,
So hallow'd and so gracious is the time.

It also started to fade when the cock crowed.
Some say, at Christmas, the rooster crows all night long,
and ghosts, fairies, and witches are too fearful to work,
because the time is so sacred.

[handwritten: some sort of spiritual connection with the crow]

HORATIO
Do you agree we should tell Hamlet about the ghost?
So have I heard and do in part believe it.
But, look, the morn, in russet mantle clad,
Walks o'er the dew of yon high eastward hill:
Break we our watch up; and by my advice,
Let us impart what we have seen to-night
Unto young Hamlet; for, upon my life,
This spirit, dumb to us, will speak to him.
Do you consent we shall acquaint him with it,
As needful in our loves, fitting our duty?

I have heard that, too, and partially believe it.
But, the morning is near, and I think we should
tell Hamlet what we have seen. The spirit does not know us,
but I bet my life, he will speak to him.
Do you agree we should tell Hamlet about the ghost?

[handwritten: want to warn him about the bad omen]

MARCELLUS
Let's do't, I pray; and I this morning know
Where we shall find him most conveniently.

Let's do it, and I know where he is this morning.
a most convenient place.

Exeunt

[handwritten: End of Scene]

Scene II

A room of state in the castle

Enter KING CLAUDIUS, QUEEN GERTRUDE, HAMLET, POLONIUS, LAERTES, VOLTIMAND, CORNELIUS, Lords, and Attendants

KING CLAUDIUS

Though yet of Hamlet our dear brother's death
The memory be green, and that it us befitted
To bear our hearts in grief and our whole kingdom
To be contracted in one brow of woe,
Yet so far hath discretion fought with nature
That we with wisest sorrow think on him,
Together with remembrance of ourselves.
Therefore our sometime sister, now our queen,
The imperial jointress to this warlike state,
Have we, as 'twere with a defeated joy,--
With an auspicious and a dropping eye,
With mirth in funeral and with dirge in marriage,
In equal scale weighing delight and dole,--
Taken to wife: nor have we herein barr'd
Your better wisdoms, which have freely gone
With this affair along. For all, our thanks.
Now follows, that you know, young Fortinbras,
Holding a weak supposal of our worth,
Or thinking by our late dear brother's death
Our state to be disjoint and out of frame,
Colleagued with the dream of his advantage,
He hath not fail'd to pester us with message,
Importing the surrender of those lands
Lost by his father, with all bonds of law,
To our most valiant brother. So much for him.
Now for ourself and for this time of meeting:
Thus much the business is: we have here writ
To Norway, uncle of young Fortinbras,--
Who, impotent and bed-rid, scarcely hears
Of this his nephew's purpose,--to suppress
His further gait herein; in that the levies,
The lists and full proportions, are all made
Out of his subject: and we here dispatch
You, good Cornelius, and you, Voltimand,
For bearers of this greeting to old Norway;
Giving to you no further personal power
To business with the king, more than the scope
Of these delated articles allow.
Farewell, and let your haste commend your duty.

CORNELIUS VOLTIMAND

In that and all things will we show our duty.

KING CLAUDIUS

We doubt it nothing: heartily farewell.
Exeunt VOLTIMAND and CORNELIUS
And now, Laertes, what's the news with you?
You told us of some suit; what is't, Laertes?
You cannot speak of reason to the Dane,
And loose your voice: what wouldst thou beg, Laertes,

Although we are still mourning our dear brother Hamlet's death, and the country is joined by grief, we must remember to continue on in life. It is with both sadness and joy, that I have married my sister-in-law, as you all advised. For your wisdom, I thank you. Now, as you all know, young Fortinbras thinks since the king has died, we are in vulnerable state. He has sent letters stating his desire to regain the land his father lost in battle to Hamlet. So, I have written a letter to his uncle, the poor bed-ridden fellow, to let him know what Fortinbras is planning. The letter asks his uncle, who in the head of Norway, to stop his nephew. I ask of you, Cornelius and Votimand, to deliver this letter and nothing else. Please be quick in fulfilling your duty.

We will do our best.

We have no doubt you will. Farewell.
(Exit Voltimand and Cornelius.)
And now, Laertes, what's new with you?
You said you had something to ask me. What is it?
Don't worry, you can ask me anything.

likely at a funeral

Gertrude ashed speechabout death and moving on with life

Sending the two to deliver the letter

Claudius says he can be trusted

12

That shall not be my offer, not thy asking?
The head is not more native to the heart,
The hand more instrumental to the mouth,
Than is the throne of Denmark to thy father.
What wouldst thou have, Laertes?

Your father is an important man to the throne of Denmark.
What do you want to ask?

LAERTES
My dread lord,
Your leave and favour to return to France;
From whence though willingly I came to Denmark,
To show my duty in your coronation,
Yet now, I must confess, that duty done,
My thoughts and wishes bend again toward France
And bow them to your gracious leave and pardon.

[handwritten: *false — originally from France?*]

I would like to ask you, if I may return to France.
Since, I came from France for the sole purpose of attending
your coronation, and with that duty done, would like to return.
Please let me go back to France.

KING CLAUDIUS
Have you your father's leave? What says Polonius?

Do you have your father's permission? What does Polonius say
about this?

LORD POLONIUS
He hath, my lord, wrung from me my slow leave
By laboursome petition, and at last
Upon his will I seal'd my hard consent:
I do beseech you, give him leave to go.

[handwritten: *Polonius is the father of Laertes*]

I have given him permission after he asked and asked.
So, I ask you to allow him to return to France.

KING CLAUDIUS
Take thy fair hour, Laertes; time be thine,
And thy best graces spend it at thy will!
But now, my cousin Hamlet, and my son,--

Then, I agree, too. This is the best time in your life,
Laertes, spend it as you will. Now, my nephew, Hamlet,
and my son--

HAMLET
[Aside]
A little more than kin, and less than kind.

I am more kin than I am kind.

KING CLAUDIUS
How is it that the clouds still hang on you?

[handwritten: *great use of diction*]

Why are you still sad? You look like a cloud is hanging over
your head.

HAMLET
Not so, my lord; I am too much i' the sun.

That's not true, sir. I am in the sun quite a bit.

QUEEN GERTRUDE
Good Hamlet, cast thy nighted colour off,
And let thine eye look like a friend on Denmark.
Do not for ever with thy vailed lids
Seek for thy noble father in the dust:
Thou know'st 'tis common; all that lives must die,
Passing through nature to eternity.

[handwritten: *says to move on from his fathers death*]

Dear Hamlet, you must stop being so dark and depressed.
It's time you rejoin the living. You cannot bring your father
back, as every living thing must die and enter eternity.

HAMLET
Ay, madam, it is common.

Yes, ma'am. I know.

QUEEN GERTRUDE
If it be,
Why seems it so particular with thee?

If you know, then why does it seem you don't?

HAMLET
Seems, madam! nay it is; I know not 'seems.'
'Tis not alone my inky cloak, good mother,
Nor customary suits of solemn black,
Nor windy suspiration of forced breath,
No, nor the fruitful river in the eye,
Nor the dejected 'havior of the visage,

[handwritten: *claims he is not faking it*]

Seems, mother! It does not seem; it is.
I may wear black clothes or behave sadly,
but I do it because I am sad, not because I am pretending to be
sad.

Together with all forms, moods, shapes of grief,
That can denote me truly: these indeed seem,
For they are actions that a man might play:
But I have that within which passeth show;
These but the trappings and the suits of woe.

KING CLAUDIUS
the best member of our court, my nephew and son.

'Tis sweet and commendable in your nature, Hamlet,
To give these mourning duties to your father:
But, you must know, your father lost a father;
That father lost, lost his, and the survivor bound
In filial obligation for some term
To do obsequious sorrow: but to persever
In obstinate condolement is a course
Of impious stubbornness; 'tis unmanly grief;
It shows a will most incorrect to heaven,
A heart unfortified, a mind impatient,
An understanding simple and unschool'd:
For what we know must be and is as common
As any the most vulgar thing to sense,
Why should we in our peevish opposition
Take it to heart? Fie! 'tis a fault to heaven,
A fault against the dead, a fault to nature,
To reason most absurd: whose common theme
Is death of fathers, and who still hath cried,
From the first corse till he that died to-day,
'This must be so.' We pray you, throw to earth
This unprevailing woe, and think of us
As of a father: for let the world take note,
You are the most immediate to our throne;
And with no less nobility of love
Than that which dearest father bears his son,
Do I impart toward you. For your intent
In going back to school in Wittenberg,
It is most retrograde to our desire:
And we beseech you, bend you to remain
Here, in the cheer and comfort of our eye,
Our chiefest courtier, cousin, and our son.

It is natural and proper for you to grieve over your father.
Everyone loses a father, and the loved ones are sorrowful
for some time. You have taken your mourning period too far.
You are showing yourself to be stubborn and unmanly.
You are going against the very nature of heaven and acting
like a simple-minded, uneducated fool. It is a sin,
continuing to act like this, so stop being so sad.
We want you to think of me as your father, since you
are heir to the throne. We want everyone to see that I love you
like a son. We do not want you to go back to school in
Wittenberg, but stay here where we can keep an eye on you,
the best member of our court, my nephew and son.

[handwritten: Says Hamlet is acting simple-minded mourning the death for too long]

[handwritten: he is the heir to King Claudius throne]

QUEEN GERTRUDE
Let not thy mother lose her prayers, Hamlet:
I pray thee, stay with us; go not to Wittenberg.

I pray you stay with us, Hamlet.
Do not go back to Wittenberg.

HAMLET
I shall in all my best obey you, madam.

I will do my best to not disappoint you, mother.

KING CLAUDIUS
Why, 'tis a loving and a fair reply:
Be as ourself in Denmark. Madam, come;
This gentle and unforced accord of Hamlet
Sits smiling to my heart: in grace whereof,
No jocund health that Denmark drinks to-day,
But the great cannon to the clouds shall tell,
And the king's rouse the heavens all bruit again,
Re-speaking earthly thunder. Come away.

That's a good answer: you are a true Dane.
Dear wife, come. I am so happy with Hamlet's decision,
I would like to drink a toast to his health.
Let's tell all of Denmark the happy news.
Let's shout it to the heavens. Let's go.

[handwritten: happy that he intends on staying]

Exeunt all but HAMLET

HAMLET

O, that this too too solid flesh would melt
Thaw and resolve itself into a dew!

Or that the Everlasting had not fix'd
His canon 'gainst self-slaughter! O God! God!
How weary, stale, flat and unprofitable,
Seem to me all the uses of this world!
Fie on't! ah fie! 'tis an unweeded garden,
That grows to seed; things rank and gross in nature
Possess it merely. That it should come to this!
But two months dead: nay, not so much, not two:
So excellent a king; that was, to this,
Hyperion to a satyr; so loving to my mother
That he might not beteem the winds of heaven
Visit her face too roughly. Heaven and earth!
Must I remember? why, she would hang on him,
As if increase of appetite had grown
By what it fed on: and yet, within a month--
Let me not think on't--Frailty, thy name is woman!--
A little month, or ere those shoes were old
With which she follow'd my poor father's body,
Like Niobe, all tears:--why she, even she--
O, God! a beast, that wants discourse of reason,
Would have mourn'd longer--married with my uncle,
My father's brother, but no more like my father
Than I to Hercules: within a month:
Ere yet the salt of most unrighteous tears
Had left the flushing in her galled eyes,
She married. O, most wicked speed, to post
With such dexterity to incestuous sheets!
It is not nor it cannot come to good:
But break, my heart; for I must hold my tongue.

I feel as though my flesh will melt.
I wish that God did not view suicide as a sin!

Oh, God! Oh, God! This world is so unfair and it seems so useless. Damn this world! Damn, this world like a garden that grows weeds. How did it come to this? My father has only been dead two months, not even two months. He was so loving to my mother. He never raised a hand to her, and she clung to him; yet, within a month... I can't even think of it! Frailty is a woman. My shoes are not even a month old. She forgets my poor father and replaces him with another. An animal without reason would have mourned longer. She should not have married my uncle, my father's brother, who is no more like my father than I am like Hercules. Within a month, the salt of her tears had not even left her eyes, and she remarried. She sped with ease to make a bed of incest which can come to no good. But, even though it breaks my heart, I must hold my tongue!

[handwritten annotations: "he is ino a mental dismay with thoughts of suicide"; "allusion of the heroic figure of Hercules"]

Enter HORATIO, MARCELLUS, and BERNARDO

HORATIO
Hail to your lordship!

Hello, my lord!

HAMLET
I am glad to see you well:
Horatio,--or I do forget myself.

I am glad to see you are doing well, Horatio.

[handwritten annotation: "He works for Hamlet"]

HORATIO
The same, my lord, and your poor servant ever.

I feel the same, my lord. I am forever your poor servant.

HAMLET
Sir, my good friend; I'll change that name with you:
And what make you from Wittenberg, Horatio? Marcellus?

Sir, my good friend, I'll change places with you.
Horatio and Marcellus, what is going on in Wittenberg?

MARCELLUS
My good lord--

My good lord...

HAMLET
I am very glad to see you. Good even, sir.
But what, in faith, make you from Wittenberg?

I am very happy to see you. Very happy.
But, tell me what is going on in Wittenberg.

HORATIO
A truant disposition, good my lord.

We are too late my lord.

[handwritten annotation: "Is Wittenberg in distress?"]

HAMLET
I would not hear your enemy say so,

I don't think you enemy would say that,

Nor shall you do mine ear that violence,
To make it truster of your own report

Against yourself: I know you are no truant.
But what is your affair in Elsinore?
We'll teach you to drink deep ere you depart.

HORATIO
My lord, I came to see your father's funeral.

HAMLET
I pray thee, do not mock me, fellow-student;
I think it was to see my mother's wedding.

HORATIO
Indeed, my lord, it follow'd hard upon.

HAMLET
Thrift, thrift, Horatio! the funeral baked meats
Did coldly furnish forth the marriage tables.
Would I had met my dearest foe in heaven
Or ever I had seen that day, Horatio!
My father!--methinks I see my father.

HORATIO
Where, my lord?

HAMLET
In my mind's eye, Horatio.

HORATIO
I saw him once; he was a goodly king.

HAMLET
He was a man, take him for all in all,
I shall not look upon his like again.

HORATIO
My lord, I think I saw him yesternight.

HAMLET
Saw? who?

HORATIO
My lord, the king your father.

HAMLET
The king my father!

HORATIO
Season your admiration for awhile
With an attent ear, till I may deliver,
Upon the witness of these gentlemen,
This marvel to you.

HAMLET
For God's love, let me hear.

HORATIO
Two nights together had these gentlemen,
Marcellus and Bernardo, on their watch,

[handwritten: Interesting line]
[handwritten: So the mother married Claudius]
[handwritten: wanted to die than see the wedding]
[handwritten: from scene 1]
[handwritten: Very set on hearing the story]

so I don't want to hear it, either.
You are never too late.

Why are you here in Elsinore? We'll teach you how to drink before you leave.

My lord, I came to attend your father's funeral.

Don't insult me. I think you came to see my mother's wedding.

True, my lord, the wedding did happen quickly after the death of your father.

Too quickly, Horatio! The food prepared for the funeral was served on the wedding tables. I would rather have died than live to see that day, Horatio! My father, I think I see him.

Where, my lord?

Only in my imagination, Horatio.

I saw him once. He was a good king.

He was a man, one like I will never meet again.

My lord, I think I saw him last night.

Saw who?

My lord, the king, your father.

The king, my father!

Hold on. Don't get so excited, until you hear the whole crazy story, witnessed by these gentlemen.

For the love of God, tell me.

These gentlemen,
Marcellus and Bernardo, on their watch

In the dead vast and middle of the night,
Been thus encounter'd. A figure like your father,
Armed at point exactly, cap-a-pe,
Appears before them, and with solemn march
Goes slow and stately by them: thrice he walk'd
By their oppress'd and fear-surprised eyes,
Within his truncheon's length; whilst they, distilled
Almost to jelly with the act of fear,
Stand dumb and speak not to him. This to me
In dreadful secrecy impart they did;
And I with them the third night kept the watch;
Where, as they had deliver'd, both in time,
Form of the thing, each word made true and good,
The apparition comes: I knew your father;
These hands are not more like.

dressed and looked like the dad

in the middle of the night, were encountered by a figure like your father. It was armed and dressed exactly like him, and marched in front of their frightened eyes. They did not speak to him because they were so afraid. So, they told me about it and I went with them last night to keep watch. Just like they reported, I saw the apparition. I knew your father, and the ghost looked just like him.

HAMLET
But where was this?

But, where was this?

MARCELLUS
My lord, upon the platform where we watch'd.

My lord, from the platform where they keep watch.

HAMLET
Did you not speak to it?

still a silent ghost

Did you speak to it?

HORATIO
My lord, I did;
But answer made it none: yet once methought
It lifted up its head and did address
Itself to motion, like as it would speak;
But even then the morning cock crew loud,
And at the sound it shrunk in haste away,
And vanish'd from our sight.

*I did, my lord.
But it did not answer. Although, I thought it lifted up its head and acted as if it were going to speak. Then, the morning cock crowed and the ghost quickly walked away and vanished from our sight.*

HAMLET
'Tis very strange.

This is very strange.

HORATIO
As I do live, my honour'd lord, 'tis true;
And we did think it writ down in our duty
To let you know of it.

wants him to know it is true

*It is, but it is true, my lord.
We thought it our duty to let you know.*

HAMLET
Indeed, indeed, sirs, but this troubles me.
Hold you the watch to-night?

*Yes, indeed, gentlemen, but this troubles me.
Are you on watch tonight?*

MARCELLUS BERNARDO
We do, my lord.

Yes, my lord.

HAMLET
Arm'd, say you?

And you say he wore his armor?

MARCELLUS BERNARDO
Arm'd, my lord.

Yes, my lord.

very curious about the armour

HAMLET
From top to toe?

From head to toe.

MARCELLUS BERNARDO
My lord, from head to foot.

My lord, completely.

HAMLET
Then saw you not his face?

Then you didn't see his face.

HORATIO
O, yes, my lord; he wore his beaver up.

Oh, yes, my lord. He wore his helmet up.

HAMLET
What, look'd he frowningly?

Did he look angry?

HORATIO
A countenance more in sorrow than in anger.

He looked more sad than angry.

HAMLET
Pale or red?

Was he pale or red?

Interesting detail to add

HORATIO
Nay, very pale.

He was very pale.

HAMLET
And fix'd his eyes upon you?

And he looked right at you?

HORATIO
Most constantly.

He stared at us.

HAMLET
I would I had been there.

I wish I would have been there.

HORATIO
It would have much amazed you.

You would have been amazed.

HAMLET
Very like, very like. Stay'd it long?

Likely so. Did it stay long?

HORATIO
While one with moderate haste might tell a hundred.

Only a few minutes.

MARCELLUS BERNARDO
Longer, longer.

It was longer than that.

HORATIO
Not when I saw't.

I don't think so.

HAMLET
His beard was grizzled--no?

Was his beard gray?

Sort of confirming it being the father

HORATIO
It was, as I have seen it in his life,
A sable silver'd.

It was just as I remember it, a silvery gray.

HAMLET
I will watch to-night;
Perchance 'twill walk again.

I will watch tonight and perhaps it will walk again.

HORATIO
I warrant it will.

I think it will.

HAMLET
If it assume my noble father's person,
I'll speak to it, though hell itself should gape
And bid me hold my peace. I pray you all,
If you have hitherto conceal'd this sight,

If it looks like my noble father,
I'll speak to it even if it is a sin and I should be quiet.
I ask you if you have not told anyone else, to keep this a secret.
Also, whatever happens tonight must remain between us. I

18

Let it be tenable in your silence still; *[wants to keep the ghost, dad thing a secret]*
And whatsoever else shall hap to-night,
Give it an understanding, but no tongue:
I will requite your loves. So, fare you well:
Upon the platform, 'twixt eleven and twelve,
I'll visit you.

All
Our duty to your honour.

HAMLET
Your loves, as mine to you: farewell.

Exeunt all but HAMLET

My father's spirit in arms! all is not well;
I doubt some foul play: would the night were come!
Till then sit still, my soul: foul deeds will rise,
Though all the earth o'erwhelm them, to men's eyes.

Exit

thinks his appearance is a bad omen

require your faithfulness. So, goodbye. I will see you at the platform between eleven and twelve.

It is our duty and our honor.

It is my honor, too. Goodbye.

My father's spirit in arms! It must mean things are not well and something terrible has happened. I wish the night were here. Until then, I must wait patiently. Bad things are surely coming.

Scene III

A room in Polonius' house

Enter LAERTES and OPHELIA

LAERTES
My necessaries are embark'd: farewell:
And, sister, as the winds give benefit
And convoy is assistant, do not sleep,
But let me hear from you.

*It is time for me to return home,
but do keep in touch, sister.*

OPHELIA
Do you doubt that?

Do you doubt that I will?

LAERTES
For Hamlet and the trifling of his favour,
Hold it a fashion and a toy in blood,
A violet in the youth of primy nature,
Forward, not permanent, sweet, not lasting,
The perfume and suppliance of a minute; No more.

*Do not believe Hamlet's ramblings of love. It is not permanent.
It is sweet, but not everlasting. It will only last a minute.*

OPHELIA
No more but so?

So what?

LAERTES
Think it no more;
For nature, crescent, does not grow alone
In thews and bulk, but, as this temple waxes,
The inward service of the mind and soul
Grows wide withal. Perhaps he loves you now,
And now no soil nor cautel doth besmirch
The virtue of his will: but you must fear,
His greatness weigh'd, his will is not his own;
For he himself is subject to his birth:
He may not, as unvalued persons do,
Carve for himself; for on his choice depends
The safety and health of this whole state;
And therefore must his choice be circumscribed
Unto the voice and yielding of that body
Whereof he is the head. Then if he says he loves you,
It fits your wisdom so far to believe it
As he in his particular act and place
May give his saying deed; which is no further
Than the main voice of Denmark goes withal.
Then weigh what loss your honour may sustain,
If with too credent ear you list his songs,
Or lose your heart, or your chaste treasure open
To his unmaster'd importunity.
Fear it, Ophelia, fear it, my dear sister,
And keep you in the rear of your affection,
Out of the shot and danger of desire.
The chariest maid is prodigal enough,
If she unmask her beauty to the moon:
Virtue itself 'scapes not calumnious strokes:
The canker galls the infants of the spring,
Too oft before their buttons be disclosed,
And in the morn and liquid dew of youth

*It is natural for him to feel the way he does.
Although, he is next in line to be king and he is beginning to
think of the people of this state as his responsibility.
He must prove his love to the queen mother to keep peace
throughout the land. It is safer to be cautious, and lose his love.
Just be weary, my dear sister, he is young and his ways are still
inconsistent and unknown.*

[handwritten annotations:]
Ophelia and Laertes are Siblings
worries of Hamlets false love
he is one significant figure of the state
↳ Personification of virtue

20

Contagious blastments are most imminent.
Be wary then; best safety lies in fear:
Youth to itself rebels, though none else near.

OPHELIA
I shall the effect of this good lesson keep,
As watchman to my heart. But, good my brother,
Do not, as some ungracious pastors do,
Show me the steep and thorny way to heaven;
Whiles, like a puff'd and reckless libertine,
Himself the primrose path of dalliance treads,
And recks not his own rede.

I shall keep what you say in mind.
But, good brother, do not tell me one thing and turn around and do something else.

[handwritten: She accepts his advice]

LAERTES
O, fear me not.
I stay too long: but here my father comes.

Oh, you need not fear me.
I have stayed too long; here comes my father.

Enter POLONIUS

A double blessing is a double grace,
Occasion smiles upon a second leave.

I am doubly blessed. It is time for me to leave.

LORD POLONIUS
Yet here, Laertes! aboard, aboard, for shame!
The wind sits in the shoulder of your sail,
And you are stay'd for. There; my blessing with thee!
And these few precepts in thy memory
See thou character. Give thy thoughts no tongue,
Nor any unproportioned thought his act.
Be thou familiar, but by no means vulgar.
Those friends thou hast, and their adoption tried,
Grapple them to thy soul with hoops of steel;
But do not dull thy palm with entertainment
Of each new-hatch'd, unfledged comrade. Beware
Of entrance to a quarrel, but being in,
Bear't that the opposed may beware of thee.
Give every man thy ear, but few thy voice;
Take each man's censure, but reserve thy judgment.
Costly thy habit as thy purse can buy,
But not express'd in fancy; rich, not gaudy;
For the apparel oft proclaims the man,
And they in France of the best rank and station
Are of a most select and generous chief in that.
Neither a borrower nor a lender be;
For loan oft loses both itself and friend,
And borrowing dulls the edge of husbandry.
This above all: to thine ownself be true,
And it must follow, as the night the day,
Thou canst not then be false to any man.
Farewell: my blessing season this in thee!

Are you still here, Laertes? Shame on you!
Everything is ready for your departure and you are still in Fortinbras. There, I give you my blessing! Keep these thoughts in mind. Be careful what you say and how you act. Be friendly, but not too friendly. Keep your old friends close, and be careful how you make new friends. Do not be quick to argue, but do not let anyone take you for a coward. Listen to your fellow man, but do not believe everything you hear. Dress your best, but do not overspend on fancy or gaudy clothes. Even the French dress according to their station. Do not borrow or lend money, because you will always lose, either the money or the friend or your sense of pride. And, most importantly, be true to yourself. That way no one can accuse you of being fake. Farewell and know you have my blessing!

[handwritten: Seems to want Laertes to leave]

[handwritten: Stay true to not be called fake]

LAERTES
Most humbly do I take my leave, my lord.

I am most humble as I leave, my lord.

LORD POLONIUS
The time invites you; go; your servants tend.

It is time. Go ahead. Your servants are waiting.

LAERTES
Farewell, Ophelia; and remember well
What I have said to you.

Goodbye, Ophelia, and remember what I said.

OPHELIA

[handwritten: Concerned for Ophelia]

'Tis in my memory lock'd,
And you yourself shall keep the key of it.

It is locked in my memory and only you have the key to unlock it.

LAERTES
Farewell.

Goodbye.

an interesting metaphor?

Exit

LORD POLONIUS
What is't, Ophelia, be hath said to you?

What did he say to you, Ophelia?

OPHELIA
So please you, something touching the Lord Hamlet.

If you must know, he said something about Lord Hamlet.

LORD POLONIUS
Marry, well bethought:
'Tis told me, he hath very oft of late *q*
Given private time to you; and you yourself
Have of your audience been most free and bounteous:
If it be so, as so 'tis put on me,
And that in way of caution, I must tell you,
You do not understand yourself so clearly
As it behoves my daughter and your honour.
What is between you? give me up the truth.

Just as I thought.
I have been told he has been spending time with you.
But, I must tell you be careful and protect yourself.
What is going on between you? Tell me the truth.

wants to know what is happening

OPHELIA
He hath, my lord, of late made many tenders
Of his affection to me.

He has, my lord, shown me how much he loves me, lately.

LORD POLONIUS
Affection! pooh! you speak like a green girl,
Unsifted in such perilous circumstance.
Do you believe his tenders, as you call them?

Love! That's worthless! You sound like a foolish girl who has no experience with danger. Do you believe him?

against their love

OPHELIA
I do not know, my lord, what I should think.

I don't know what to think, my lord.

LORD POLONIUS
Marry, I'll teach you: think yourself a baby;
That you have ta'en these tenders for true pay,
Which are not sterling. Tender yourself more dearly;
Or--not to crack the wind of the poor phrase,
Running it thus--you'll tender me a fool.

Love! That's worthless! You sound like a foolish girl who has no experience with danger. Do you believe him?

OPHELIA
My lord, he hath importuned me with love
In honourable fashion.

Father, he has treated me with love in an honorable fashion.

she thinks the love is true

LORD POLONIUS
Ay, fashion you may call it; go to, go to.

Yes, you can call it fashion, something that changes often. Go ahead.

OPHELIA
And hath given countenance to his speech, my lord,
With almost all the holy vows of heaven.

He swears he is being honest.

LORD POLONIUS
Ay, springes to catch woodcocks. I do know,
When the blood burns, how prodigal the soul
Lends the tongue vows: these blazes, daughter,
Giving more light than heat, extinct in both,
Even in their promise, as it is a-making,

Bologna! I know when lust burns in the blood, how quickly one is to take vows of any kind. His heart may burn for you, but do not be deceived by what stokes the fire. Act like a grown woman and don't believe Lord Hamlet's vows. Do not be alone with him anymore. I demand you listen to me and change your ways.

You must not take for fire. From this time
Be somewhat scanter of your maiden presence;
Set your entreatments at a higher rate
Than a command to parley. For Lord Hamlet,
Believe so much in him, that he is young
And with a larger tether may he walk
Than may be given you: in few, Ophelia,
Do not believe his vows; for they are brokers,
Not of that dye which their investments show,
But mere implorators of unholy suits,
Breathing like sanctified and pious bawds,
The better to beguile. This is for all:
I would not, in plain terms, from this time forth,
Have you so slander any moment leisure,
As to give words or talk with the Lord Hamlet.
Look to't, I charge you: come your ways.

OPHELIA
I shall obey, my lord.

I will obey, my lord.

Exeunt

Metaphorically saying not to believe a word that comes out of Hamlet's mouth

Interesting choice of scene

Scene IV

The platform

Enter HAMLET, HORATIO, and MARCELLUS

HAMLET
The air bites shrewdly; it is very cold.

The air is bitterly cold.

HORATIO
It is a nipping and an eager air.

It is nippy in the air.

[handwritten: personification to show how cold it is]

HAMLET
What hour now?

What time is it now?

HORATIO
I think it lacks of twelve.

I think it is almost twelve.

IIAMLET
No, it is struck.

No, it is already struck twelve.

HORATIO
Indeed? I heard it not: then it draws near the season
Wherein the spirit held his wont to walk.

It is? I didn't hear it. Then, the time is near for the spirit to hold his walk.

A flourish of trumpets, and ordnance shot off, within

What does this mean, my lord?

What is that? What does it mean, my lord?

HAMLET
The king doth wake to-night and takes his rouse,
Keeps wassail, and the swaggering up-spring reels;
And, as he drains his draughts of Rhenish down,
The kettle-drum and trumpet thus bray out
The triumph of his pledge.

It means the king is awake tonight and is up drinking. The drum and trumpet play to show a pledge to be triumphant.

[handwritten: gives context to the reader]

HORATIO
Is it a custom?

Is it a custom?

HAMLET
Ay, marry, is't:
But to my mind, though I am native here
And to the manner born, it is a custom
More honour'd in the breach than the observance.
This heavy-headed revel east and west
Makes us traduced and tax'd of other nations:
They clepe us drunkards, and with swinish phrase
Soil our addition; and indeed it takes
From our achievements, though perform'd at height,
The pith and marrow of our attribute.
So, oft it chances in particular men,
That for some vicious mole of nature in them,
As, in their birth--wherein they are not guilty,
Since nature cannot choose his origin--
By the o'ergrowth of some complexion,
Oft breaking down the pales and forts of reason,
Or by some habit that too much o'er-leavens
The form of plausive manners, that these men,

*Yes, it is.
But, although I am from here, I don't think it is a good one. Many countries think we are drunks. They do not think we are capable of great achievements, like someone who is born with an affliction they cannot control or someone with a bad habit. It is unfortunate, but people are judged by these things. A little problem can mar a whole man's life.*

[handwritten: doesn't like being judged and accused of drunks]

Carrying, I say, the stamp of one defect,
Being nature's livery, or fortune's star,--
Their virtues else--be they as pure as grace,
As infinite as man may undergo--
Shall in the general censure take corruption
From that particular fault: the dram of eale
Doth all the noble substance of a doubt
To his own scandal.

HORATIO
Look, my lord, it comes!

[handwritten: Will it be his father?]

Enter Ghost

Look, my lord, here it comes!

HAMLET
Angels and ministers of grace defend us!
Be thou a spirit of health or goblin damn'd,
Bring with thee airs from heaven or blasts from hell,
Be thy intents wicked or charitable,
Thou comest in such a questionable shape
That I will speak to thee: I'll call thee Hamlet,
King, father, royal Dane: O, answer me!
Let me not burst in ignorance; but tell
Why thy canonized bones, hearsed in death,
Have burst their cerements; why the sepulchre,
Wherein we saw thee quietly inurn'd,
Hath oped his ponderous and marble jaws,
To cast thee up again. What may this mean,
That thou, dead corse, again in complete steel
Revisit'st thus the glimpses of the moon,
Making night hideous; and we fools of nature
So horridly to shake our disposition
With thoughts beyond the reaches of our souls?
Say, why is this? wherefore? what should we do?

God help us! Whether you are an angel or demon, from heaven or hell, good or bad, I will speak to you. I'll call you Hamlet, King, father, royal Dane. Oh, answer me! Tell me why you are here. What does it mean the dead walking? Why are you in your battle armor and making us doubt our minds? Why? What do you want?

[handwritten: Hamlet wants to know everything about the ghost]

Ghost beckons HAMLET

HORATIO
It beckons you to go away with it,
As if it some impartment did desire
To you alone.

[handwritten: Wants a private moment]

It beckons for you to go with it, as if it wants to be with you alone.

MARCELLUS
Look, with what courteous action
It waves you to a more removed ground:
But do not go with it.

Look, it wants you to go over there, but don't go!

HORATIO
No, by no means.

No, by no means.

HAMLET
It will not speak; then I will follow it.

It will not speak, if I don't follow.

HORATIO
Do not, my lord.

[handwritten: Horatio thinks following it is a bad idea]

Do not, my lord.

HAMLET
Why, what should be the fear?
I do not set my life in a pin's fee;
And for my soul, what can it do to that,
Being a thing immortal as itself?

*Why not? What do I have to fear?
It cannot hurt me or take my soul.
It waves at me, again. I'll follow.*

It waves me forth again: I'll follow it.

HORATIO
What if it tempt you toward the flood, my lord,
Or to the dreadful summit of the cliff
That beetles o'er his base into the sea,
And there assume some other horrible form,
Which might deprive your sovereignty of reason
And draw you into madness? think of it:
The very place puts toys of desperation,
Without more motive, into every brain
That looks so many fathoms to the sea
And hears it roar beneath.

*What if it tempts you toward the water, my lord,
or to the end of the cliff or assumes some other horrible form
which drives you insane.*

HAMLET
It waves me still.
Go on; I'll follow thee.

It still waves at me. Go on. I'll follow you.

MARCELLUS
You shall not go, my lord.

You will not, my lord.

HAMLET
Hold off your hands.

Take your hands off of me.

HORATIO
Be ruled; you shall not go.

Be sensible. You will not go.

HAMLET
My fate cries out,
And makes each petty artery in this body
As hardy as the Nemean lion's nerve.
Still am I call'd. Unhand me, gentlemen.
By heaven, I'll make a ghost of him that lets me!
I say, away! Go on; I'll follow thee.

*This is my fate and I am not afraid.
Now, take your hands off, gentlemen. I swear, I'll make a ghost
of you, if you don't. I say, go on. I'll follow you.*

Exeunt Ghost and HAMLET

HORATIO
He waxes desperate with imagination.

He is desperate and not thinking sensibly.

MARCELLUS
Let's follow; 'tis not fit thus to obey him.

Let's follow him. It is not right for us to let him go alone.

HORATIO
Have after. To what issue will this come?

Go ahead. What good can come of this?

MARCELLUS
Something is rotten in the state of Denmark.

Something terrible is definitely happening in Denmark.

HORATIO
Heaven will direct it.

God will protect him.

MARCELLUS
Nay, let's follow him.

No, let's follow him.

Exeunt

[Handwritten annotations:]
the ghost could lead him to go mad
thinks that he has no choice
still thinks it is all a bad sign

SCENE V

Another part of the platform.

Enter GHOST and HAMLET

HAMLET
Where wilt thou lead me? speak; I'll go no further.

Where are you leading me? Speak or I'll stop.

Ghost
Mark me.

Listen to me.

HAMLET
I will.

the ghost speaks!

I will.

Ghost
My hour is almost come,
When I to sulphurous and tormenting flames
Must render up myself.

*My time is almost up,
and I have to return to the sulfurous fire and tormenting flames.*

HAMLET
Alas, poor ghost!

You poor ghost!

Ghost
Pity me not, but lend thy serious hearing
To what I shall unfold.

Hamlet must listen to the ghost

Don't pity me, but listen to what I have to say.

HAMLET
Speak; I am bound to hear.

Speak. I am listening.

Ghost
So art thou to revenge, when thou shalt hear.

You will want revenge when you hear my story.

HAMLET
What?

What?

Ghost
I am thy father's spirit,
Doom'd for a certain term to walk the night,
And for the day confined to fast in fires,
Till the foul crimes done in my days of nature
Are burnt and purged away. But that I am forbid
To tell the secrets of my prison-house,
I could a tale unfold whose lightest word
Would harrow up thy soul, freeze thy young blood,
Make thy two eyes, like stars, start from their spheres,
Thy knotted and combined locks to part
And each particular hair to stand on end,
Like quills upon the fretful porpentine:
But this eternal blazon must not be
To ears of flesh and blood. List, list, O, list!
If thou didst ever thy dear father love--

confirms that it is the father

*I am the spirit of your father,
and I am doomed to walk the night and confined by day to waste
in the fires, until I have paid for the crimes of my life. But, I am
forbidden to tell the secrets of hell, although I could tell a small
story that would freeze your blood, make your eyes pop out of
your head, or make your hair stand on end like the quills of a
porcupine. However, I cannot tell you. Listen, if you ever loved
your dear father--*

HAMLET
O God!

similie of a porc- upine

Oh, God!

Ghost
Revenge his foul and most unnatural murder.

You will seek revenge for his foul murder.

HAMLET
Murder!

Ghost
Murder most foul, as in the best it is;
But this most foul, strange and unnatural.

HAMLET
Haste me to know't, that I, with wings as swift
As meditation or the thoughts of love,
May sweep to my revenge.

Ghost
I find thee apt;
And duller shouldst thou be than the fat weed
That roots itself in ease on Lethe wharf,
Wouldst thou not stir in this. Now, Hamlet, hear:
'Tis given out that, sleeping in my orchard,
A serpent stung me; so the whole ear of Denmark
Is by a forged process of my death
Rankly abused: but know, thou noble youth,
The serpent that did sting thy father's life
Now wears his crown.

HAMLET
O my prophetic soul! My uncle!

Ghost
Ay, that incestuous, that adulterate beast,
With witchcraft of his wit, with traitorous gifts,--
O wicked wit and gifts, that have the power
So to seduce!--won to his shameful lust
The will of my most seeming-virtuous queen:
O Hamlet, what a falling-off was there!
From me, whose love was of that dignity
That it went hand in hand even with the vow
I made to her in marriage, and to decline
Upon a wretch whose natural gifts were poor
To those of mine!
But virtue, as it never will be moved,
Though lewdness court it in a shape of heaven,
So lust, though to a radiant angel link'd,
Will sate itself in a celestial bed,
And prey on garbage.
But, soft! methinks I scent the morning air;
Brief let me be. Sleeping within my orchard,
My custom always of the afternoon,
Upon my secure hour thy uncle stole,
With juice of cursed hebenon in a vial,
And in the porches of my ears did pour
The leperous distilment; whose effect
Holds such an enmity with blood of man
That swift as quicksilver it courses through
The natural gates and alleys of the body,
And with a sudden vigour doth posset
And curd, like eager droppings into milk,
The thin and wholesome blood: so did it mine;
And a most instant tetter bark'd about,
Most lazar-like, with vile and loathsome crust,
All my smooth body.
Thus was I, sleeping, by a brother's hand

Murder!

Yes, murder, in the most unnatural sense.

Hurry and tell me, so I can seek revenge quickly.

I know you are capable and no one would suspect you. Now, listen Hamlet. It was told throughout Denmark that while I was sleeping in my orchard, I was bitten by a serpent, but I want you to the serpent that bit me now wears my crown.

I knew it! My uncle!

Yes, that incestuous beast of adultery and witchcraft. He is traitorous and has the powers of seduction, which won him my most seemingly virtuous queen. Oh, Hamlet, what a terrible blow. My wife, whom I loved with dignity from the day we married, falls for the likes of him. But, perhaps her virtue was not as solid as I thought to fall so quickly into the bed of another. Wait! I think the morning is approaching, and I must be brief. Your uncle, while I was sleeping in the orchard like every afternoon, came and poured some poison into my ear. The poison worked quickly and my body became crusty with death, and I was not given the opportunity to confess my sins. Oh, horrible! Horrible! Most horrible! Protect yourself against sin, and however you go about getting your revenge, leave your mother alone. Let heaven deal with her. Living with the truth will prick and sting her enough. Now, I must go. The sun is rising. Goodbye. Goodbye. Hamlet, remember me!

revealed his cause of death

did Claudius kill the past King.

upset that his wife may decided to wed with King Claudius

Of life, of crown, of queen, at once dispatch'd:
Cut off even in the blossoms of my sin,
Unhousel'd, disappointed, unanel'd,
No reckoning made, but sent to my account
With all my imperfections on my head:
O, horrible! O, horrible! most horrible!
If thou hast nature in thee, bear it not;
Let not the royal bed of Denmark be
A couch for luxury and damned incest.
But, howsoever thou pursuest this act,
Taint not thy mind, nor let thy soul contrive
Against thy mother aught: leave her to heaven
And to those thorns that in her bosom lodge,
To prick and sting her. Fare thee well at once!
The glow-worm shows the matin to be near,
And 'gins to pale his uneffectual fire:
Adieu, adieu! Hamlet, remember me.

wants him to leave it to faith to punish her

Exit

HAMLET
O all you host of heaven! O earth! what else?
And shall I couple hell? O, fie! Hold, hold, my heart;
And you, my sinews, grow not instant old,
But bear me stiffly up. Remember thee!
Ay, thou poor ghost, while memory holds a seat
In this distracted globe. Remember thee!
Yea, from the table of my memory
I'll wipe away all trivial fond records,
All saws of books, all forms, all pressures past,
That youth and observation copied there;
And thy commandment all alone shall live
Within the book and volume of my brain,
Unmix'd with baser matter: yes, by heaven!
O most pernicious woman!
O villain, villain, smiling, damned villain!
My tables,--meet it is I set it down,
That one may smile, and smile, and be a villain;
At least I'm sure it may be so in Denmark:

Hamlet is clearly very upset about hearing this news

Oh, God of heaven and earth! What else can I bear? I swear! Be still, my heart and body give me strength. Remember you! You poor ghost, I will remember you. I will think of nothing else. Oh, villainous woman! Oh, villain, damned villain! How can one sit and smile and know he is a villain? I know it is possible in Denmark.

Writing

So, uncle, there you are. Now to my word;
It is 'Adieu, adieu! remember me.'
I have sworn 't.

So, uncle, there you are. I will keep my word and remember my father. I have sworn it.

MARCELLUS HORATIO
[Within]
My lord, my lord,--

My lord, my lord,--

MARCELLUS
[Within]
Lord Hamlet,--

Lord Hamlet,--

HORATIO
[Within]
Heaven secure him!

many religious allusions

Heaven protect him!

HAMLET
So be it!

So be it!

HORATIO
[Within]
Hillo, ho, ho, my lord!

Hello, my lord!

HAMLET
Hillo, ho, ho, boy! come, bird, come.

Hello, boy! Come here, come.

Enter HORATIO and MARCELLUS

MARCELLUS
How is't, my noble lord?

How are you, my noble lord?

HORATIO
What news, my lord?

What happened, my lord?

HAMLET
O, wonderful!

It was wonderful!

Interesting term to use as his reaction

HORATIO
Good my lord, tell it.

Good my lord, tell us.

HAMLET
No; you'll reveal it.

No, you'll tell someone.

HORATIO
Not I, my lord, by heaven.

Not me, my lord, I swear.

MARCELLUS
Nor I, my lord.

Nor me, my lord.

HAMLET
How say you, then; would heart of man once think it?
But you'll be secret?

Can you keep a secret?

HORATIO MARCELLUS
Ay, by heaven, my lord.

Yes, we swear, my lord.

HAMLET
There's ne'er a villain dwelling in all Denmark
But he's an arrant knave.

There's a villain living in Denmark, an awful scoundrel.

HORATIO
There needs no ghost, my lord, come from the grave
To tell us this.

No ghost needed to tell us that, my lord.

they were right

HAMLET
Why, right; you are i' the right;
And so, without more circumstance at all,
I hold it fit that we shake hands and part:
You, as your business and desire shall point you;
For every man has business and desire,
Such as it is; and for mine own poor part,
Look you, I'll go pray.

You are so right. So, I think we should shake hands and go our separate ways, you to your business and me, well, I need to go pray.

HORATIO
These are but wild and whirling words, my lord.

You aren't making much sense, my lord.

HAMLET
I'm sorry they offend you, heartily;
Yes, 'faith heartily.

I'm sorry they offend you. I truly am.

Hamlet is not making sense to them

HORATIO

There's no offence, my lord.

I'm not offended, my lord.

HAMLET
Yes, by Saint Patrick, but there is, Horatio,
And much offence too. Touching this vision here,
It is an honest ghost, that let me tell you:
For your desire to know what is between us,
O'ermaster 't as you may. And now, good friends,
As you are friends, scholars and soldiers,
Give me one poor request.

Oh, but there has been an offense, I swear by Saint Patrick, Horatio. From what the honest ghost says, a large offense, too. I know you want to know what was said, but I must keep it to myself. Now, good friends, you are friends, scholars, and soldiers; I ask but one thing.

Horatio can't know the secret

HORATIO
What is't, my lord? we will.

What is it, my lord? We will.

HAMLET
Never make known what you have seen to-night.

Never tell anyone what you have seen tonight.

HORATIO MARCELLUS
My lord, we will not.

My lord, we will not tell anyone.

HAMLET
Nay, but swear't.

No, swear it.

HORATIO
In faith,
My lord, not I.

I swear, my lord, I will never tell.

MARCELLUS
Nor I, my lord, in faith.

really set on keeping this a secret

Nor I, my lord, I swear.

HAMLET
Upon my sword. →

Swear upon my sword.

MARCELLUS
We have sworn, my lord, already.

We have already sworn, my lord.

HAMLET
Indeed, upon my sword, indeed.

You have, but I want you to swear upon my sword.

Ghost
[Beneath]
Swear.

Swear.

HAMLET
Ah, ha, boy! say'st thou so? art thou there, truepenny?
Come on--you hear this fellow in the cellarage--
Consent to swear.

Ha, ha boy! Is that right? Aren't you helpful?
Come on! You hear the fellow down below. Swear.

HORATIO
Propose the oath, my lord.

Say the oath, my lord.

HAMLET
Never to speak of this that you have seen,
Swear by my sword.

Swear by my sword, you will never speak of what you have seen.

Ghost
[Beneath]
Swear.

Still forcing them to promise

Swear.

HAMLET

Hic et ubique? then we'll shift our ground.
Come hither, gentlemen,
And lay your hands again upon my sword:
Never to speak of this that you have heard,
Swear by my sword.

Ghost
[Beneath]
Swear.

→ *Interesting to include*

HAMLET
Well said, old mole! canst work i' the earth so fast?
A worthy pioner! Once more remove, good friends.

HORATIO
O day and night, but this is wondrous strange!

HAMLET
And therefore as a stranger give it welcome.
There are more things in heaven and earth, Horatio,
Than are dreamt of in your philosophy. But come;
Here, as before, never, so help you mercy,
How strange or odd soe'er I bear myself,
As I perchance hereafter shall think meet
To put an antic disposition on,
That you, at such times seeing me, never shall,
With arms encumber'd thus, or this headshake,
Or by pronouncing of some doubtful phrase,
As 'Well, well, we know,' or 'We could, an if we would,'
Or 'If we list to speak,' or 'There be, an if they might,'
Or such ambiguous giving out, to note
That you know aught of me: this not to do,
So grace and mercy at your most need help you, Swear.

no matter what,
Horatio can't
say anything

Ghost
[Beneath]
Swear.

HAMLET
Rest, rest, perturbed spirit!
So, gentlemen,
With all my love I do commend me to you:
And what so poor a man as Hamlet is
May do, to express his love and friending to you,
God willing, shall not lack. Let us go in together;
And still your fingers on your lips, I pray.
The time is out of joint: O cursed spite,
That ever I was born to set it right!
Nay, come, let's go together.

Exeunt

Hamlet's
greatest
secret

He is everywhere. Let's move.
Come over here, gentlemen,
and lay your hands upon my sword.
Swear you will never tell anyone what you have heard.
Swear by my sword.

Swear.

Well said, old mole! I wished I could move that fast.
He is a worthy pioneer! Try again, good friends.

I swear this is weird.

Yes, it is strange, but you want to know. First, there are more things in heaven and earth, Horatio, than you know about. But, listen to what I am about to say. No matter how I act or what I say, and undoubtedly, I will act crazy and say inane things in the future, you must not let on you know what is going on. You may never say, "Oh, just as I thought," or "If you only knew." Swear it!

Swear.

Rest, poor spirit.
So, gentlemen,
I give you all my love and will repay you for your friendship.
Let's go back inside together, but you must stay quiet, please.
You must not talk about any of this.
I know it is extremely strange, and I curse the day I am supposed to set everything straight. Come on, let's go inside.

Act II

Interested to see
how it will connect
to Act I

Scene I

A room in POLONIUS' house

Enter POLONIUS and REYNALDO

LORD POLONIUS
Give him this money and these notes, Reynaldo.

Give him this money and these notes, Reynaldo.

REYNALDO
I will, my lord.

I will, my lord.

LORD POLONIUS
You shall do marvellous wisely, good Reynaldo,
Before you visit him, to make inquire
Of his behavior.

It would be wise, Reynaldo,
before you visit him, to find out what he's been up to.

REYNALDO
My lord, I did intend it. →7 I think he
is the servant

Those were my intentions, my lord.

LORD POLONIUS
Marry, well said; very well said. Look you, sir, to lord
Inquire me first what Danskers are in Paris; Polonius
And how, and who, what means, and where they keep,
What company, at what expense; and findin
By this encompassment and drift of question
That they do know my son, come you more nearer
Than your particular demands will touch it:
Take you, as 'twere, some distant knowledge of him;
As thus, 'I know his father and his friends,
And in part him: ' do you mark this, Reynaldo?

Good, well said.
Ask around and find out what Danes are in Paris—who they are,
where they live, how they make money and who their friends
are? Also, find out if they know my son. You will find out more
by asking these questions than if you enquired directly about
him. Just say you are a friend of his father and vaguely know
him. Understand, Reynaldo?

REYNALDO
Ay, very well, my lord.

No problem, sir.

LORD POLONIUS
'And in part him; but' you may say 'not well:
But, if't be he I mean, he's very wild;
Addicted so and so:' and there put on him
What forgeries you please; marry, none so rank
As may dishonour him; take heed of that;
But, sir, such wanton, wild and usual slips
As are companions noted and most known
To youth and liberty.

And you may make up stories about him like he acts wildly or
likes to drink, et cetera, but don't make up anything that would
be shameful. You know, make up something believable about
someone of his age and position.

Can lie, but do not degrade him

REYNALDO
As gaming, my lord.

Like gambling?

LORD POLONIUS
Ay, or drinking, fencing, swearing, quarrelling,
Drabbing: you may go so far.

Yes, or drinking, fencing, swearing, fighting,
or visiting brothels.

REYNALDO
My lord, that would dishonour him.

But that would bring him shame.

LORD POLONIUS
'Faith, no; as you may season it in the charge
You must not put another scandal on him,

Oh, heavens no, not if you say it the right way. You may say
what you need to but do not make him seem scandalous.

It's all about the phrasing

That he is open to incontinency;
That's not my meaning: but breathe his faults so quaintly
That they may seem the taints of liberty,
The flash and outbreak of a fiery mind,
A savageness in unreclaimed blood,
Of general assault.

Just mention his faults in a way that seem usual of someone like Laertes, a fiery youth from a long-line of fiery men.

make up lies to confuse them

REYNALDO

But, my good lord,--

But, my good sir--

LORD POLONIUS

Wherefore should you do this?

You want to know why I want you to do this?

REYNALDO

Ay, my lord,
I would know that.

Yes, my lord, I would.

LORD POLONIUS

Marry, sir, here's my drift;
And I believe, it is a fetch of wit:
You laying these slight sullies on my son,
As 'twere a thing a little soil'd i' the working, Mark you,
Your party in converse, him you would sound,
Having ever seen in the prenominate crimes
The youth you breathe of guilty, be assured
He closes with you in this consequence;
'Good sir,' or so, or 'friend,' or 'gentleman,'
According to the phrase or the addition
Of man and country.

Okay, sir, this is what I think and if I say so myself, it is very clever. I think if you mention my son's faults in vague conversation as if it was nothing, the other person will agree with you saying, 'Yes, my good sir,' or 'No, my friend.'

vagueness of Laertes will lead to agreement

REYNALDO

Very good, my lord.

I understand, my lord.

LORD POLONIUS

And then, sir, does he this--he does--what was I
about to say? By the mass, I was about to say
something: where did I leave?

And then sir, he will—what was I about to say?—Good lord, I was about to say something. Where did I leave off?

Is he forgetful?

REYNALDO

At 'closes in the consequence,' at 'friend or so,'
and 'gentleman.'

You were saying how the other person would respond.

LORD POLONIUS

At 'closes in the consequence,' ay, marry;
He closes thus: 'I know the gentleman;
I saw him yesterday, or t' other day,
Or then, or then; with such, or such; and, as you say,
There was a' gaming; there o'ertook in's rouse;
There falling out at tennis:' or perchance,
'I saw him enter such a house of sale,'
Videlicet, a brothel, or so forth.
See you now;
Your bait of falsehood takes this carp of truth:
And thus do we of wisdom and of reach,
With windlasses and with assays of bias,
By indirections find directions out:
So by my former lecture and advice,
Shall you my son. You have me, have you not?

Oh yes, the other person. He'll say, "Yes, I know that gentlemen; I saw him yesterday. He was gambling or he was fighting." You see what I mean? See, your little lie will actually reveal the truth. That's how you'll find out what Laertes is doing in Paris. Understand?

a white lie will reveal a great truth

REYNALDO

My lord, I have.

I understand, sir.

LORD POLONIUS
God be wi' you; fare you well.

May God be with you.

REYNALDO
Good my lord!

Thank you, my lord!

LORD POLONIUS
Observe his inclination in yourself.

Don't forget to observe his actions for yourself.

REYNALDO
I shall, my lord.

I will, sir.

LORD POLONIUS
And let him ply his music.

Make sure he is studying his music.

REYNALDO
Well, my lord.

No problem, sir.

LORD POLONIUS
Farewell!

Goodbye!

Exit REYNALDO

Enter OPHELIA

How now, Ophelia! what's the matter?

Ophelia, what is wrong?

OPHELIA
O, my lord, my lord, I have been so affrighted!

Oh, father, I have been so scared!

LORD POLONIUS
With what, i' the name of God?

By what, in the name of God?

OPHELIA
My lord, as I was sewing in my closet,
Lord Hamlet, with his doublet all unbraced;
No hat upon his head; his stockings foul'd,
Ungarter'd, and down-gyved to his ancle;
Pale as his shirt; his knees knocking each other;
And with a look so piteous in purport
As if he had been loosed out of hell
To speak of horrors,--he comes before me.

*My lord, as I was sewing in my bedroom,
Lord Hamlet appeared. His vest was unbuttoned,
there was no hat on his head, his socks were dirty and down
around his ankles, and he was as pale as his shirt. He was
He was pitiful looking with his knees knocking together, as if he
had seen the demons in hell.*

LORD POLONIUS
Mad for thy love?

Was he insane with love for you?

OPHELIA
My lord, I do not know;
But truly, I do fear it.

I don't know, but that is what I'm afraid of.

LORD POLONIUS
What said he?

What did he say?

OPHELIA
He took me by the wrist and held me hard;
Then goes he to the length of all his arm;
And, with his other hand thus o'er his brow,
He falls to such perusal of my face
As he would draw it. Long stay'd he so;
At last, a little shaking of mine arm
And thrice his head thus waving up and down,

*He took me by the wrist with a hard grip.
Then, he holds me at arm's length and stares at me like an artist
preparing to draw a portrait. He stayed like that for so long, my
arm began to shake. He shook his head three times and sighed
so loudly and pitifully, it seemed he was about to die. Then he let
me go and without opening his eyes he left, like I was the last
thing he wanted to see.*

He raised a sigh so piteous and profound
As it did seem to shatter all his bulk
And end his being: that done, he lets me go:
And, with his head over his shoulder turn'd,
He seem'd to find his way without his eyes;
For out o' doors he went without their helps,
And, to the last, bended their light on me.

She felt un-wanted

LORD POLONIUS

Come, go with me: I will go seek the king.
This is the very ecstasy of love,
Whose violent property fordoes itself
And leads the will to desperate undertakings
As oft as any passion under heaven
That does afflict our natures. I am sorry.
What, have you given him any hard words of late?

passion has a great influence

Come on, let's go see the king.
He is acting like he is in love with you and I am afraid of what
he might do in the name of passion. I am sorry, but have you
spoken harshly to him lately?

OPHELIA

No, my good lord, but, as you did command,
I did repel his fetters and denied
His access to me.

No, father. I did as you told me.
I wouldn't receive his letters or let him visit me.

LORD POLONIUS

That hath made him mad.
I am sorry that with better heed and judgment
I had not quoted him: I fear'd he did but trifle,
And meant to wreck thee; but, beshrew my jealousy!
By heaven, it is as proper to our age
To cast beyond ourselves in our opinions
As it is common for the younger sort
To lack discretion. Come, go we to the king:
This must be known; which, being kept close, might move
More grief to hide than hate to utter love.

That is probably what made him angry. I'm sorry. I should have
monitored him more closely before I gave you such advice, but I
thought he was just trying to use you. I guess people my age
think we know more. Let's go see the king and tell him what is
going on. It is better to have this out in the open.

Polonius says sorry for misjudging Hamlet

Exeunt

Scene II

A room in the castle

Enter KING CLAUDIUS, QUEEN GERTRUDE, ROSENCRANTZ, GUILDENSTERN, and

Attendants

KING CLAUDIUS
Welcome, dear Rosencrantz and Guildenstern!
Moreover that we much did long to see you,
The need we have to use you did provoke
Our hasty sending. Something have you heard
Of Hamlet's transformation; so call it,
Sith nor the exterior nor the inward man
Resembles that it was. What it should be,
More than his father's death, that thus hath put him
So much from the understanding of himself,
I cannot dream of: I entreat you both,
That, being of so young days brought up with him,
And sith so neighbour'd to his youth and havior,
That you vouchsafe your rest here in our court
Some little time: so by your companies
To draw him on to pleasures, and to gather,
So much as from occasion you may glean,
Whether aught, to us unknown, afflicts him thus,
That, open'd, lies within our remedy.

Welcome Rosencratntz and Guildenstern.
We have looked so forward to seeing you, but we sent for you so
hastily, because we need your assistance. I'm sure you have
heard of Hamlet's "transformation," or at least that's
what I call it. He is not like he used to be. He doesn't even look
the same. I have no idea what has caused this change other than
his father's death. So, I am asking for both of you, being so close
in age to Hamlet, to stay here and spend some time with him.
Try to figure out what is wrong with him and let us know, so we
may help him.

Some sort of negative change to Hamlet

QUEEN GERTRUDE
Good gentlemen, he hath much talk'd of you;
And sure I am two men there are not living
To whom he more adheres. If it will please you
To show us so much gentry and good will
As to expend your time with us awhile,
For the supply and profit of our hope,
Your visitation shall receive such thanks
As fits a king's remembrance.

Gentlemen, Hamlet has talked so much about you,
I am sure there are no others alive to whom he is as close. If you
would be so kind to spend some time with us and help us with
Hamlet, I am sure your visit would be compensated befitting a
king.

Hamlet greatly is close to R&G

ROSENCRANTZ
Both your majesties
Might, by the sovereign power you have of us,
Put your dread pleasures more into command
Than to entreaty.

I beg your pardon, your majesties,
but knowing the power you have over us, it seems as if your
request is more of a command than a question.

GUILDENSTERN
But we both obey,
And here give up ourselves, in the full bent
To lay our service freely at your feet,
To be commanded.

It would be our pleasure to be of service.
We are at your command.

Sort of calling out the obvious

KING CLAUDIUS
Thanks, Rosencrantz and gentle Guildenstern.

Thanks, Rosencrantz and Guildenstern.

QUEEN GERTRUDE
Thanks, Guildenstern and gentle Rosencrantz:
And I beseech you instantly to visit
My too much changed son. Go, some of you,
And bring these gentlemen where Hamlet is.

Thank you, Guildenstern and gentle Rosencrantz.
I ask you to go to Hamlet, who has changed so much lately.
Attendants, some of you take these gentlemen to Hamlet.

Interesting use of repitition

GUILDENSTERN
Heavens make our presence and our practices
Pleasant and helpful to him!

May God bless us in helping Hamlet!

QUEEN GERTRUDE
Ay, amen!

Amen!

Exeunt ROSENCRANTZ, GUILDENSTERN, and some Attendants

Enter POLONIUS

LORD POLONIUS
The ambassadors from Norway, my good lord,
Are joyfully return'd.

I see the ambassadors from Norway have happily returned.

[handwritten: disputes of countries]

KING CLAUDIUS
Thou still hast been the father of good news.

You are still the bearer of good news.

LORD POLONIUS
Have I, my lord? I assure my good liege,
I hold my duty, as I hold my soul,
Both to my God and to my gracious king:
And I do think, or else this brain of mine
Hunts not the trail of policy so sure
As it hath used to do, that I have found
The very cause of Hamlet's lunacy.

Am I, my lord? I assure you I take my duty to the King as seriously as my soul to God. I think I know what may be wrong with Hamlet and causing him to act so crazily.

[handwritten: does he know about the ghost?]

KING CLAUDIUS
O, speak of that; that do I long to hear.

Do tell me what I long to hear.

LORD POLONIUS
Give first admittance to the ambassadors;
My news shall be the fruit to that great feast.

*First, let me get the ambassadors.
My news will be the cherry on top of what they have to say.*

[handwritten: great metaphor]

KING CLAUDIUS
Thyself do grace to them, and bring them in.

Sure. Bring them in.

Exit POLONIUS

He tells me, my dear Gertrude, he hath found
The head and source of all your son's distemper.

Polonius tells me, my sweet queen, he may know what is wrong with your son.

QUEEN GERTRUDE
I doubt it is no other but the main;
His father's death, and our o'erhasty marriage.

I doubt it is anything other than the death of his father and our hasty marriage.

[handwritten: thinks its obvious]

KING CLAUDIUS
Well, we shall sift him.

Well, we will hear him out.

Re-enter POLONIUS, with VOLTIMAND and CORNELIUS

Welcome, my good friends!
Say, Voltimand, what from our brother Norway?

*Welcome, good friends!
What do you know, Voltimand, about our neighbor Norway?*

VOLTIMAND
Most fair return of greetings and desires.
Upon our first, he sent out to suppress
His nephew's levies; which to him appear'd
To be a preparation 'gainst the Polack;
But, better look'd into, he truly found

Thank you, your highness. When we first visited Norway, your brother sent out soldiers to stop his nephew. He thought Fortinbras was preparing to attack the Poles, but at a second look, he discovered the attack was meant for you. This news made him sick, so he arrested Fortinbras, who in turn, vowed to

It was against your highness: whereat grieved,
That so his sickness, age and impotence
Was falsely borne in hand, sends out arrests
On Fortinbras; which he, in brief, obeys;
Receives rebuke from Norway, and in fine
Makes vow before his uncle never more
To give the assay of arms against your majesty.
Whereon old Norway, overcome with joy,
Gives him three thousand crowns in annual fee,
And his commission to employ those soldiers,
So levied as before, against the Polack:
With an entreaty, herein further shown,

his uncle to not send arms against Denmark. His uncle, being so overjoyed by his nephew's vows, gave him an increase in his annual salary and permission to employ soldiers to attack the Poles.

Is Polack Poland?

Giving a paper
That it might please you to give quiet pass
Through your dominions for this enterprise,
On such regards of safety and allowance
As therein are set down.

He asks for safe passage through Denmark for this mission.

he needs a safe way to get to Denmark

KING CLAUDIUS
It likes us well;
And at our more consider'd time well read,
Answer, and think upon this business.
Meantime we thank you for your well-took labour:
Go to your rest; at night we'll feast together:
Most welcome home!

I think that will be fine but I will read it later and make my decision. In the meantime, thank you for your work. Go get some rest for tonight we will feast together. Welcome home!

Exeunt VOLTIMAND and CORNELIUS

LORD POLONIUS
This business is well ended.
My liege, and madam, to expostulate
What majesty should be, what duty is,
Why day is day, night night, and time is time,
Were nothing but to waste night, day and time.
Therefore, since brevity is the soul of wit,
And tediousness the limbs and outward flourishes,
I will be brief: your noble son is mad:
Mad call I it; for, to define true madness,
What is't but to be nothing else but mad?
But let that go.

Well, that turned out well. My liege and madam, to think about what is majestic, what duty is, why day is day, night is night, and time is time, is a waste of time. To be serious for a moment, and I will be brief, I think your son is crazy. I call it crazy, because I don't know a better word to describe his actions. But, let's put madness aside.

Plainly calls Hamlet insane

QUEEN GERTRUDE
More matter, with less art.

Get to the point and don't embellish the truth.

LORD POLONIUS
Madam, I swear I use no art at all.
That he is mad, 'tis true: 'tis true 'tis pity;
And pity 'tis 'tis true: a foolish figure;
But farewell it, for I will use no art.
Mad let us grant him, then: and now remains
That we find out the cause of this effect,
Or rather say, the cause of this defect,
For this effect defective comes by cause:
Thus it remains, and the remainder thus. Perpend.
I have a daughter--have while she is mine--
Who, in her duty and obedience, mark,
Hath given me this: now gather, and surmise.

Madam, I swear I am telling the truth. Hamlet is mad. It is pitiful and true. I am not embellishing the truth. If he is mad, and I think he is, then we must find the cause of his craziness, because it must be caused by something. You see, I have a daughter, for now, who is dutiful and obedient in giving me this. Now listen and see what you think.

love this way of saying to find the truth

Reads

'To the celestial and my soul's idol, the most beautiful Ophelia,'—	*"To the heavenly idol of my soul, the most beautiful Ophelia,"—*
That's an ill phrase, a vile phrase; 'beautified' is a vile phrase: but you shall hear. Thus:	*That's a little forward and calling her beautiful is definitely bold. But listen.*
Reads	
'In her excellent white bosom, these, & c.'	*"In her excellent white bosom, et cetera."*

(handwritten: this means etcetera)

QUEEN GERTRUDE

Came this from Hamlet to her?	*Hamlet sent this to her?*

LORD POLONIUS

Good madam, stay awhile; I will be faithful.	*Yes madam, listen for there is more.*

Reads

'Doubt thou the stars are fire; Doubt that the sun doth move; Doubt truth to be a liar; But never doubt I love.	*"You may doubt the stars are made of fire, the sun moves, or truth is a liar, but never doubt my love for you.*
'O dear Ophelia, I am ill at these numbers; I have not art to reckon my groans: but that I love thee best, O most best, believe it. Adieu. 'Thine evermore most dear lady, whilst this machine is to him, HAMLET.' This, in obedience, hath my daughter shown me, And more above, hath his solicitings, As they fell out by time, by means and place, All given to mine ear.	*"Oh dear Ophelia, I am not good at putting my feelings into words, but know I love you best, the best of all. Believe it. Goodbye." "Yours truly, my dear lady, as long as I live." My daughter in her obedience gave me this letter and told me how he has wooed her.*

(handwritten: Hamlet's letter to Ophilio)

KING CLAUDIUS

But how hath she Received his love?	*How does she feel about him?*

LORD POLONIUS

What do you think of me?	*What do you take me for?*

KING CLAUDIUS

As of a man faithful and honourable.	*I think you are a faithful and honorable man.*

LORD POLONIUS

I would fain prove so. But what might you think, When I had seen this hot love on the wing-- As I perceived it, I must tell you that, Before my daughter told me--what might you, Or my dear majesty your queen here, think, If I had play'd the desk or table-book, Or given my heart a winking, mute and dumb, Or look'd upon this love with idle sight; What might you think? No, I went round to work, And my young mistress thus I did bespeak: 'Lord Hamlet is a prince, out of thy star; This must not be:' and then I precepts gave her, That she should lock herself from his resort, Admit no messengers, receive no tokens. Which done, she took the fruits of my advice; And he, repulsed--a short tale to make-- Fell into a sadness, then into a fast, Thence to a watch, thence into a weakness,	*I should hope so. But, what would you have thought of me if I had turned my head when I saw this blossoming love? What would you or your majesty the queen thought if I had not acted on what I saw? No, I took action. I told my daughter, "Lord Hamlet is a prince and not of your same position in life." Then, I ordered her to stay away from him, take no messages from him, or any gifts. When she did this, he fell into such a sadness that he could not eat, which led to a weak state that turned into madness. All of this took place while we were preoccupied by the situation with Fortinbras.*

(handwritten: Wants them to honor Lord Polonius' word)

Thence to a lightness, and, by this declension,
Into the madness wherein now he raves,
And all we mourn for.

KING CLAUDIUS
Do you think 'tis this?

Do you think this is possible?

QUEEN GERTRUDE
It may be, very likely.

It is possible and quite possible.

LORD POLONIUS
Hath there been such a time--I'd fain know that--
That I have positively said 'Tis so,'
When it proved otherwise?

Have I ever told you something I thought was true and it turned out not to be?

when have I ever let you down?!

KING CLAUDIUS
Not that I know.

Not that I know of.

LORD POLONIUS
[Pointing to his head and shoulder]

Take this from this, if this be otherwise:
If circumstances lead me, I will find
Where truth is hid, though it were hid indeed
Within the centre.

Not that I know of.
If it is not the truth, I will find out what is if I have to go the center of the world.

KING CLAUDIUS
How may we try it further?

What can we do to find out?

LORD POLONIUS
You know, sometimes he walks four hours together
Here in the lobby.

Sometimes he walks for hours here in the lobby.

QUEEN GERTRUDE
So he does indeed.

He does indeed.

LORD POLONIUS
At such a time I'll loose my daughter to him:
Be you and I behind an arras then;
Mark the encounter: if he love her not
And be not from his reason fall'n thereon,
Let me be no assistant for a state,
But keep a farm and carters.

he will use Ophelia as bait

When he is walking, I will allow my daughter to go to him. We will hide and watch what happens. If he doesn't love her and his love is not the reason for his breakdown then I will no longer be an assistant for the state, but a farmer.

KING CLAUDIUS
We will try it.

Okay, we will try it.

QUEEN GERTRUDE
But, look, where sadly the poor wretch comes reading.

Here he comes, the sad fellow, walking and reading.

LORD POLONIUS
Away, I do beseech you, both away:
I'll board him presently.

Go. Both of you go away and I'll talk to him.

Exeunt KING CLAUDIUS, QUEEN GERTRUDE, and Attendants

Enter HAMLET, reading → *what is he reading?*

O, give me leave:
How does my good Lord Hamlet?

How are you Hamlet?

HAMLET

Well, God-a-mercy.

I'm well, thanks be to God.

LORD POLONIUS
Do you know me, my lord?

Do you recognize me, my lord?

HAMLET
Excellent well; you are a fishmonger.

Of course; you're a fishmonger.

LORD POLONIUS
Not I, my lord.

No, not me, my lord.

HAMLET
Then I would you were so honest a man.

Well, I hope you are an honest man.

LORD POLONIUS
Honest, my lord!

Oh yes, I am honest, sir.

HAMLET
Ay, sir; to be honest, as this world goes, is to be
one man picked out of ten thousand.

Yes, it is rare to be honest in this world.
Only one out of ten thousand men are honest.

LORD POLONIUS
That's very true, my lord.

That's very true, my lord.

HAMLET
For if the sun breed maggots in a dead dog, being a
god kissing carrion,--Have you a daughter?

For if the sun causes maggots in a dead dog,--
Have you a daughter?

LORD POLONIUS
I have, my lord.

I do, my lord.

HAMLET
Let her not walk i' the sun: conception is a
blessing: but not as your daughter may conceive.
Friend, look to 't.

Don't let her walk in the sun. Conception is a blessing, but don't
let your daughter conceive that way, friend.

LORD POLONIUS
[Aside]
How say you by that? Still harping on my
daughter: yet he knew me not at first; he said I
was a fishmonger: he is far gone, far gone: and
truly in my youth I suffered much extremity for
love; very near this. I'll speak to him again.
What do you read, my lord?

What do you mean? He is still hung up on my daughter. Yet, he
didn't know me at first. He thought I was a fishmonger. He is far
gone, and I remember suffering from love's sting in my youth.
I'll try to talk to him again. What are you reading, my lord?

HAMLET
Words, words, words.

Words, words, words.

LORD POLONIUS
What is the matter, my lord?

What is the matter, my lord?

HAMLET
Between who?

Between who?

LORD POLONIUS
I mean, the matter that you read, my lord.

I mean, the subject matter that you read, my lord.

HAMLET
Slanders, sir: for the satirical rogue says here
that old men have grey beards, that their faces are

Lies, sir. The slave to satire says here
that old men have gray beards and wrinkled faces,

[handwritten: What is a fishmonger?]

[handwritten: very few people are honest]

[handwritten: I think Hamlet truly loves Ophelia]

[handwritten: Interesting to state that he is reading words]

wrinkled, their eyes purging thick amber and
plum-tree gum and that they have a plentiful lack of
wit, together with most weak hams: all which, sir,
though I most powerfully and potently believe, yet
I hold it not honesty to have it thus set down, for
yourself, sir, should be old as I am, if like a crab
you could go backward.

*their cloudy eyes are blood-shot, and they have lost their minds
as well as their strength. Although, I believe it to be true, I think
it is wrong to write it down.*
*Don't you agree, you being as old as I am, if you could go back
in time?*

LORD POLONIUS
[Aside]
Though this be madness, yet there is method in 't.
Will you walk out of the air, my lord?

*There is some sense in his madness. Will you come outside, my
lord?*

[handwritten: fancy way to say that there is method to his madness]

HAMLET
Into my grave.

To my grave?

LORD POLONIUS
Indeed, that is out o' the air.

Well, that is outside.

Aside

How pregnant sometimes his replies are! a happiness
that often madness hits on, which reason and sanity
could not so prosperously be delivered of. I will
leave him, and suddenly contrive the means of
meeting between him and my daughter.--My honourable
lord, I will most humbly take my leave of you.

*He seems to be hinting at something with his answers. He seems
so happy, too; a happiness only possible through insanity. I will
leave him and arrange a later meeting between him and my
daughter.—My honorable lord, I am leaving now.*

[handwritten: strangely happy]

HAMLET
You cannot, sir, take from me any thing that I will
more willingly part withal: except my life, except
my life, except my life.

*You cannot, sir. Take anything from me except my life, except my
life, except my life.*

LORD POLONIUS
Fare you well, my lord.

Goodbye, my lord.

HAMLET
These tedious old fools!

These are some worrisome old fools!

Enter ROSENCRANTZ and GUILDENSTERN

LORD POLONIUS
You go to seek the Lord Hamlet; there he is.

If you are looking for the Lord Hamlet, he is over there.

ROSENCRANTZ
[To POLONIUS]
God save you, sir!

Thank you, sir!

Exit POLONIUS

GUILDENSTERN
My honoured lord!

My honored lord!

[handwritten: very happy to see them]

ROSENCRANTZ
My most dear lord!

My most dear sir!

HAMLET
My excellent good friends! How dost thou,
Guildenstern? Ah, Rosencrantz! Good lads, how do ye both?

*Well, look who it is, my excellent friends! How are you,
Guildenstern? And, Rosencrantz! Gentlemen, how are you?*

ROSENCRANTZ

As the indifferent children of the earth.

We are well, happy and carefree.

GUILDENSTERN
Happy, in that we are not over-happy;
On fortune's cap we are not the very button.

Happy, but not overly happy. We have been lucky, but not the luckiest.

[handwritten: saying they are doing fine]

HAMLET
Nor the soles of her shoe?

But, you haven't been unlucky?

ROSENCRANTZ
Neither, my lord.

No, we are fine.

HAMLET
Then you live about her waist, or in the middle of her favours?

So you live about the waist of Lady Luck.

GUILDENSTERN
'Faith, her privates we.

Yes, by God, we live somewhere in the middle.

[handwritten: Personifying luck]

HAMLET
In the secret parts of fortune? O, most true; she is a strumpet. What's the news?

Near her secret parts? Oh, she is a whore. What's going on?

ROSENCRANTZ
None, my lord, but that the world's grown honest.

Nothing, my lord, since there is peace in the world.

HAMLET
Then is doomsday near; but your news is not true.
Let me question more in particular: what have you,
my good friends, deserved at the hands of fortune,
that she sends you to prison hither?

I guess that means that the end of the world is soon. Let me be more specific: What are doing here in this prison?

[handwritten: peace only means eventual downfall]

GUILDENSTERN
Prison, my lord!

Prison, my lord!

HAMLET
Denmark's a prison.

Denmark's a prison.

ROSENCRANTZ
Then is the world one.

So is the world.

[handwritten: that way deep]

HAMLET
A goodly one; in which there are many confines,
wards and dungeons, Denmark being one o' the worst.

Yes, the world has many prisons, and Denmark is the worst.

ROSENCRANTZ
We think not so, my lord.

We don't think so, my lord.

HAMLET
Why, then, 'tis none to you; for there is nothing
either good or bad, but thinking makes it so: to me
it is a prison.

Well, you may not think so, but it is definitely a prison to me.

ROSENCRANTZ
Why then, your ambition makes it one; 'tis too
narrow for your mind.

That is because you are so ambitious. You are too big for such a small country.

[handwritten: frowns upon Denmark greatly]

HAMLET
O God, I could be bounded in a nut shell and count
myself a king of infinite space, were it not that I

Oh, God, I could live in a nut shell and feel like a king, but I have bad dreams.

have bad dreams.

GUILDENSTERN
Which dreams indeed are ambition, for the very
substance of the ambitious is merely the shadow of a dream.

Dreams and ambition are one in the same; ambition is the shadow of a dream.

HAMLET
A dream itself is but a shadow.

A dream is just a shadow.

ROSENCRANTZ
Truly, and I hold ambition of so airy and light a
quality that it is but a shadow's shadow.

That is true that I think a dream is just a shadow of a shadow.

HAMLET
Then are our beggars bodies, and our monarchs and
outstretched heroes the beggars' shadows. Shall we
to the court? for, by my fay, I cannot reason.

In that case, beggars are real and kings or heroes are the shadows of beggars. Let's go inside. I can't think anymore.

ROSENCRANTZ GUILDENSTERN
We'll wait upon you.

We're waiting on you.

HAMLET
No such matter: I will not sort you with the rest
of my servants, for, to speak to you like an honest
man, I am most dreadfully attended. But, in the
beaten way of friendship, what make you at Elsinore?

No way. I will not put you with the rest of my servants, because they are dreadful. But, tell me friends, why are you in Elsinore?

ROSENCRANTZ
To visit you, my lord; no other occasion.

Just to visit you, my lord; no other reason.

HAMLET
Beggar that I am, I am even poor in thanks; but I
thank you: and sure, dear friends, my thanks are
too dear a halfpenny. Were you not sent for? Is it
your own inclining? Is it a free visitation? Come,
deal justly with me: come, come; nay, speak.

I am a beggar now and am poor in thanks, but, I thank you. My thanks are not even worth very much. Weren't you sent for? Or was it your own decision? Is this visitation without some purpose? Just tell me, straight.

GUILDENSTERN
What should we say, my lord?

What do you want us to say, my lord?

HAMLET
Why, any thing, but to the purpose. You were sent
for; and there is a kind of confession in your looks
which your modesties have not craft enough to colour:
I know the good king and queen have sent for you.

Tell me whatever you wish, but answer my question. You were sent for. I can tell by the look on your face. You are not good at lying. I know the good king and queen sent for you.

ROSENCRANTZ
To what end, my lord?

Why would they do that, my lord?

HAMLET
That you must teach me. But let me conjure you, by
the rights of our fellowship, by the consonancy of
our youth, by the obligation of our ever-preserved
love, and by what more dear a better proposer could
charge you withal, be even and direct with me,
whether you were sent for, or no?

You tell me. But let me remind you of our friendship, starting in our youth, and our love for one another. Tell me directly, if you were sent for.

ROSENCRANTZ
[Aside to GUILDENSTERN]
What say you?

What should we say?

(handwritten margin notes: "a very profound statement" · "also very profound" · "he wants to know the truth" · "reminds them of being close friends")

HAMLET
[Aside]
Nay, then, I have an eye of you.--If you
love me, hold not off.

I am watching you.—If you love me, don't lie.

GUILDENSTERN
My lord, we were sent for.

My lord, we were sent for.

HAMLET
I will tell you why; so shall my anticipation
prevent your discovery, and your secrecy to the king
and queen moult no feather. I have of late—but
wherefore I know not--lost all my mirth, forgone all
custom of exercises; and indeed it goes so heavily
with my disposition that this goodly frame, the
earth, seems to me a sterile promontory, this most
excellent canopy, the air, look you, this brave
o'erhanging firmament, this majestical roof fretted
with golden fire, why, it appears no other thing to
me than a foul and pestilent congregation of vapours.
What a piece of work is a man! how noble in reason!
how infinite in faculty! in form and moving how
express and admirable! in action how like an angel!
in apprehension how like a god! the beauty of the
world! the paragon of animals! And yet, to me,
what is this quintessence of dust? man delights not
me: no, nor woman neither, though by your smiling
you seem to say so.

tells the truth

Well, I will tell you why you were asked to come. Then, your allegiance to the king and queen will not be broken. Lately, I have been depressed. You know, lost my zeal for life. I did not want to exercise or have any fun. The world is just a foul place. And, man! What a joke! I have no interest in men or manly things, or women, for that matter. I guess you still do, by the smile on your face.

Pitying himself, no interest in anyone anymore

ROSENCRANTZ
My lord, there was no such stuff in my thoughts.

I wasn't thinking anything like that.

HAMLET
Why did you laugh then, when I said 'man delights not me'?

Why did you laugh then, when I said "I do not have any in interest in things of men?"

ROSENCRANTZ
To think, my lord, if you delight not in man, what
lenten entertainment the players shall receive from
you: we coted them on the way; and hither are they
coming, to offer you service.

I was just thinking, if you don't like the things that make men happy, you're going to be pretty bored by the actors we passed on the way here. They are coming to entertain you.

Interesting to see what they will do

HAMLET
He that plays the king shall be welcome; his majesty
shall have tribute of me; the adventurous knight
shall use his foil and target; the lover shall not
sigh gratis; the humourous man shall end his part
in peace; the clown shall make those laugh whose
lungs are tickled o' the sere; and the lady shall
say her mind freely, or the blank verse shall halt
for't. What players are they?

I'll welcome the actor who plays the king and watch the knight as he waves around his weapons. I will show the lover gratitude and laugh at the clown, and I'll listen to the lady character babble on. Which actors are coming?

ROSENCRANTZ
Even those you were wont to take delight in, the
tragedians of the city.

The tragic group from the city.

HAMLET
How chances it they travel? their residence, both
in reputation and profit, was better both ways.

What are they doing on the road? They were very popular and profitable.

these are well known actors

ROSENCRANTZ
I think their inhibition comes by the means of the
late innovation.

Things change and now they travel.

HAMLET
Do they hold the same estimation they did when I was
in the city? are they so followed?

*Are they still popular as they used to be? Do they still
pull a crowd?*

ROSENCRANTZ
No, indeed, are they not. → *have lost their crowds*

No, not anymore.

HAMLET
How comes it? do they grow rusty?

Why? Are they getting old?

ROSENCRANTZ
Nay, their endeavour keeps in the wonted pace: but
there is, sir, an aery of children, little eyases,
that cry out on the top of question, and are most
tyrannically clapped for't: these are now the
fashion, and so berattle the common stages--so they *the*
call them--that many wearing rapiers are afraid of *kids essentially*
goose-quills and dare scarce come thither. *run the show*

*No, they are the same, but there is a group of children who yell
out their lines the crowd loves. They are all the rage. The rich
theater-goers don't come out for fear they will be teased by the
writers.*

HAMLET
What, are they children? who maintains 'em? how are
they escoted? Will they pursue the quality no
longer than they can sing? will they not say
afterwards, if they should grow themselves to common
players--as it is most like, if their means are no
better--their writers do them wrong, to make them
exclaim against their own succession?

*Children actors? Who takes care of them? How do they get
around? Will they stay actors when they grow up?
Won't they be used up by the time they are adults? Or do they
have money?*

ROSENCRANTZ
'Faith, there has been much to do on both sides; and
the nation holds it no sin to tarre them to
controversy: there was, for a while, no money bid
for argument, unless the poet and the player went to
cuffs in the question.

*True, there has been a lot of controversy over the subject. For
awhile, no plays were being held without a big fight over who
was going to act.*

HAMLET
Is't possible?

controversial pieces and players

Really?

GUILDENSTERN
O, there has been much throwing about of brains.

Oh, there has been much arguing about it.

HAMLET
Do the boys carry it away?

Can the boys carry it off?

ROSENCRANTZ
Ay, that they do, my lord; Hercules and his load too.

Yes, they do. And they handle an adult load, too.

HAMLET
It is not very strange; for mine uncle is king of
Denmark, and those that would make mows at him while
my father lived, give twenty, forty, fifty, an
hundred ducats a-piece for his picture in little.
'Sblood, there is something in this more than
natural, if philosophy could find it out.

*I guess it is not very strange. For example, my uncle, the king of
Denmark, was made fun of when my father lived. Now, those
same people who made fun of him are paying for a little picture
of him. It certainly is something to think about.*

Flourish of trumpets within

who was once buried now rules over

GUILDENSTERN

48

There are the players.

Here come the actors.

HAMLET
Gentlemen, you are welcome to Elsinore. Your hands,
come then: the appurtenance of welcome is fashi
and ceremony: let me comply with you in this garb,
lest my extent to the players, which, I tell you,
must show fairly outward, should more appear like
entertainment than yours. You are welcome: but my
uncle-father and aunt-mother are deceived.

*Gentlemen, welcome to Elsinore. Shake my hand and let me keep
up with fashion and customs. You are welcome. But, let me
deceive my uncle-father and aunt-mother.*

GUILDENSTERN
In what, my dear lord?

Still planning his revenge

In what, my dear lord?

HAMLET
I am but mad north-north-west: when the wind is
southerly I know a hawk from a handsaw.

*I am completely crazy, sometimes. But, other times I am straight
as an arrow.*

Enter POLONIUS

LORD POLONIUS
Well be with you, gentlemen!

Gentlemen, I hope you are well!

HAMLET
Hark you, Guildenstern; and you too: at each ear a
hearer: that great baby you see there is not yet
out of his swaddling-clouts.

*Hey, listen Guilderstern and Rosencrantz. There's a great big
baby who is still in diapers.*

ROSENCRANTZ
Happily he's the second time come to them; for they
say an old man is twice a child.

*He must be in his second childhood; once a man, twice a child,
they say.*

HAMLET
I will prophesy he comes to tell me of the players;
mark it. You say right, sir: o' Monday morning;
'twas so indeed.

an interesting saying

*I believe he is coming to tell me about the actors.
Watch. Oh, yes, you were right about Monday.*

LORD POLONIUS
My lord, I have news to tell you.

My lord, I have news for you.

HAMLET
My lord, I have news to tell you.
When Roscius was an actor in Rome,--

*My lord, I have news for you. When Roscius was an actor in
Rome...*

LORD POLONIUS
The actors are come hither, my lord.

The actors are here, my lord.

HAMLET
Buz, buz! → 'Doesn't really care'

Whatever!

LORD POLONIUS
Upon mine honour,--

My word...

HAMLET
Then came each actor on his ass,--

Each one coming in on his ass...

LORD POLONIUS
The best actors in the world, either for tragedy,
comedy, history, pastoral, pastoral-comical,
historical-pastoral, tragical-historical, tragical-

*These are the best actors in the world. They can perform
anything from Seneca to Plautus. There is nothing too difficult
for these actors.*

comical-historical-pastoral, scene individable, or
poem unlimited: Seneca cannot be too heavy, nor
Plautus too light. For the law of writ and the
liberty, these are the only men.

→ they can act anything

HAMLET
O Jephthah, judge of Israel, what a treasure hadst thou!

Oh, Jephthah, judge of Israel, what a treasure you have!

LORD POLONIUS
What a treasure had he, my lord?

What treasure are you talking about?

HAMLET
Why,
'One fair daughter and no more,
The which he loved passing well.'

another allusion

Well, "One fair daughter, and no more; that he loved so well."

LORD POLONIUS
[Aside]
Still on my daughter.

Still hung up on my daughter.

HAMLET
Am I not i' the right, old Jephthah?

Am I not telling it right, old Jephthah?

LORD POLONIUS
If you call me Jephthah, my lord, I have a daughter
that I love passing well.

I do have a daughter like Japhthath, my lord, and I love her very much.

HAMLET
Nay, that follows not.

No, that can't be right?

LORD POLONIUS
What follows, then, my lord?

What is right, then?

HAMLET
Why,
'As by lot, God wot,'
and then, you know,
'It came to pass, as most like it was,'--
the first row of the pious chanson will show you
more; for look, where my abridgement comes.

→ god only knows what is right

Why, only God knows what is right. Listen to the words. Wait, here comes the actors.

Enter four or five Players

You are welcome, masters; welcome, all. I am glad
to see thee well. Welcome, good friends. O, my old
friend! thy face is valenced since I saw thee last:
comest thou to beard me in Denmark? What, my young
lady and mistress! By'r lady, your ladyship is
nearer to heaven than when I saw you last, by the
altitude of a chopine. Pray God, your voice, like
apiece of uncurrent gold, be not cracked within the
ring. Masters, you are all welcome. We'll e'en
to't like French falconers, fly at any thing we see:
we'll have a speech straight: come, give us a taste
of your quality; come, a passionate speech.

You are welcome friends. I am glad to see you doing so well. Oh, I know you. You've grown a beard, since I saw you last. Have you come to put a beard on me, too? And, my young lady, you've grown, since I saw you. I hope your voice hasn't changed. Actors, you are welcome. Give us a speech, a passionate one to peak our interests.

First Player
What speech, my lord?

very welcoming to them

What kind of speech, my lord?

HAMLET
I heard thee speak me a speech once, but it was

I heard you once make a speech, but you never acted it out. Or if

never acted; or, if it was, not above once; for the play, I remember, pleased not the million; 'twas caviare to the general: but it was--as I received it, and others, whose judgments in such matters cried in the top of mine--an excellent play, well digested in the scenes, set down with as much modesty as cunning. I remember, one said there were no sallets in the lines to make the matter savoury, nor no matter in the phrase that might indict the author of affectation; but called it an honest method, as wholesome as sweet, and by very much more handsome than fine. One speech in it I chiefly loved: 'twas Aeneas' tale to Dido; and thereabout of it especially, where he speaks of Priam's slaughter: if it live in your memory, begin at this line: let me see, let me see--
'The rugged Pyrrhus, like the Hyrcanian beast,'-- it is not so:--it begins with Pyrrhus:--
'The rugged Pyrrhus, he whose sable arms, Black as his purpose, did the night resemble When he lay couched in the ominous horse, Hath now this dread and black complexion smear'd With heraldry more dismal; head to foot Now is he total gules; horridly trick'd With blood of fathers, mothers, daughters, sons, Baked and impasted with the parching streets, That lend a tyrannous and damned light To their lord's murder: roasted in wrath and fire, And thus o'er-sized with coagulate gore, With eyes like carbuncles, the hellish Pyrrhus Old grandsire Priam seeks.'
So, proceed you.

recalls a speech that was not acting but presented very well

LORD POLONIUS
'Fore God, my lord, well spoken, with good accent and good discretion.

tells him which one

First Player
'Anon he finds him
Striking too short at Greeks; his antique sword, Rebellious to his arm, lies where it falls, Repugnant to command: unequal match'd, Pyrrhus at Priam drives; in rage strikes wide; But with the whiff and wind of his fell sword The unnerved father falls. Then senseless Ilium, Seeming to feel this blow, with flaming top Stoops to his base, and with a hideous crash Takes prisoner Pyrrhus' ear: for, lo! his sword, Which was declining on the milky head Of reverend Priam, seem'd i' the air to stick: So, as a painted tyrant, Pyrrhus stood, And like a neutral to his will and matter, Did nothing.
But, as we often see, against some storm, A silence in the heavens, the rack stand still, The bold winds speechless and the orb below As hush as death, anon the dreadful thunder Doth rend the region, so, after Pyrrhus' pause, Aroused vengeance sets him new a-work; And never did the Cyclops' hammers fall On Mars's armour forged for proof eterne

praising Hamlet for that

it was, it wasn't very popular. It was like caviar to the poor. But, the critics and I thought it was excellent. I remember one said it was not fancy but clever. Another said it was truly honest. One speech I loved was from Aeneas to Dido, talking about the death of Priam.

If you remember it, start with "The rugged Pyrrhus, like the Hyrcanian beast." No, that's not right. It started with "The rugged Pyrrhus, with black arms and purpose, resembling the night on his horse, is now covered in red blood of fathers, mothers, daughters, and sons. The blood is baked with the burning streets from fires he lit that illuminate the murders he committed. Drenched in gore, he goes in search of old Priam." Start from there.

I swear to God, my lord, you said that so well and with the proper accent and pauses.

Soon, he finds him, after his fall to the Greeks. With his old sword he is unable to bear, young Pyrrhus drives at Priam. His rage leaves him unbalanced but the force of his blow knocks Priam to the ground. Just before taking the head of Priam, Pyrrhus hears the roar of flames in the city of Ilium. He stands frozen as if in a painting. Like the quiet before the storm, Pyrrhus took back up his sword and with newly found fury wielded a deathly blow on Priam.—Out, out Fortune, you whore. Gods of heaven, take away her power and break her wheel of fortune. Send her and it to the depths of hell.

A very interesting speech

With less remorse than Pyrrhus' bleeding sword
Now falls on Priam.
Out, out, thou strumpet, Fortune! All you gods,
In general synod 'take away her power;
Break all the spokes and fellies from her wheel,
And bowl the round nave down the hill of heaven,
As low as to the fiends!'

LORD POLONIUS
This is too long.

This is too long.

HAMLET
It shall to the barber's, with your beard. Prithee,
on: he's for a jig or a tale of bawdry, or he
sleeps: say on: come to Hecuba.

Seems a bit comedic

We'll let the barber cut it, as well as your beard.—Please go say on.—He only likes the crude scenes, or else he falls asleep.—Go to the part about Hecuba.

First Player
'But who, O, who had seen the mobled queen--'

But who had seen the quiet queen,--

HAMLET
'The mobled queen?'

The "quiet queen?"

LORD POLONIUS
That's good; 'mobled queen' is good.

That sounds good! "Quiet queen!"

First Player
'Run barefoot up and down, threatening the flames
With bisson rheum; a clout upon that head
Where late the diadem stood, and for a robe,
About her lank and all o'er-teemed loins,
A blanket, in the alarm of fear caught up;
Who this had seen, with tongue in venom steep'd,
'Gainst Fortune's state would treason have pronounced:
But if the gods themselves did see her then
When she saw Pyrrhus make malicious sport
In mincing with his sword her husband's limbs,
The instant burst of clamour that she made,
Unless things mortal move them not at all,
Would have made milch the burning eyes of heaven,
And passion in the gods.'

talks of the murder of a husband

She runs barefoot throughout the city threatening to put out the flames with her tears, a cloth on her head which once bore a crown and a blanket around her where once she wore a robe. Someone seeing her like this would have cursed Fortune. Even the gods, themselves, would have pity on her if they had seen her watch Pyrrhus murder her husband, unless the gods have no care for humans.

LORD POLONIUS
Look, whether he has not turned his colour and has
tears in's eyes. Pray you, no more.

Look, the actor has turned colors and has tears in his eyes. Please let him stop!

HAMLET
'Tis well: I'll have thee speak out the rest soon.
Good my lord, will you see the players well
bestowed? Do you hear, let them be well used; for
they are the abstract and brief chronicles of the
time: after your death you were better have a bad
epitaph than their ill report while you live.

the players took the scene to heart

Very well. I'll have you tell me the rest, soon.—Polonius, will you see the players are taken care of? Do you understand? Be good to them, for it would be better to have a bad epitaph than have them angry with you.

LORD POLONIUS
My lord, I will use them according to their desert.

My lord, I will treat them as they deserve.

HAMLET
God's bodykins, man, much better: use every man
after his desert, and who should 'scape whipping?
Use them after your own honour and dignity: the less
they deserve, the more merit is in your bounty.

Treat them well

Oh no man, if every man were treated as he deserved, no one would escape punishment. Treat them as you would want to be treated with respect and honor. The less deserving, the more the generosity. Take them inside.

Take them in.

LORD POLONIUS
Come, sirs.

Come along, sirs.

HAMLET
Follow him, friends: we'll hear a play to-morrow.

Go with him, my friends. We'll hear a play tomorrow.

Exit POLONIUS with all the Players but the First

Dost thou hear me, old friend; can you play the Murder of Gonzago?

Do you know the play, "The Murder of Gonzago?"

First Player
Ay, my lord.

all connected to murder

Yes, my lord.

HAMLET
We'll ha't to-morrow night. You could, for a need, study a speech of some dozen or sixteen lines, which I would set down and insert in't, could you not?

We would like to hear it tomorrow night. Could you add a few lines for me?

First Player
Ay, my lord.

Is this his revenge?

Yes, my lord.

HAMLET
Very well. Follow that lord; and look you mock him not.

Good.—Follow that man; and do not mock him.

Exit First Player

My good friends, I'll leave you till night: you are welcome to Elsinore.

My friends, I must leave now. I will see you tonight. Welcome to Elsinore.

ROSENCRANTZ
Good my lord!

Okay, my lord.

HAMLET
Ay, so, God be wi' ye;

Good, go with God.

Exeunt ROSENCRANTZ and GUILDENSTERN

Now I am alone.
O, what a rogue and peasant slave am I!
Is it not monstrous that this player here,
But in a fiction, in a dream of passion,
Could force his soul so to his own conceit
That from her working all his visage wann'd,
Tears in his eyes, distraction in's aspect,
A broken voice, and his whole function suiting
With forms to his conceit? and all for nothing!
For Hecuba!
What's Hecuba to him, or he to Hecuba,
That he should weep for her? What would he do,
Had he the motive and the cue for passion
That I have? He would drown the stage with tears
And cleave the general ear with horrid speech,
Make mad the guilty and appal the free,q
Confound the ignorant, and amaze indeed
The very faculties of eyes and ears. Yet I,
A dull and muddy-mettled rascal, peak,
Like John-a-dreams, unpregnant of my cause,

feels bad for showing the actor such a powerful scene

Thank God, I am alone. What a mischievous man I am! Aren't I terrible to make the actor feel something so powerful in his soul that it brought tears to his eyes and made his voice crack. And, for what? Nothing! For Hecuba? What's Hecuba to him or vice-versa? What would he do if her were in my shoes? He would probably cry and make horrible speeches, drive the guilty crazy and appall the little ones. He would confuse the ignorant spectators and amaze them. But I am not so brave and so I say nothing against a king who stole his position and property. Am I a coward? Would someone call me a villain, hit me, pull off my beard and blow it back in my face, or tweak my nose? Would someone call me a liar and I not respond? I wouldn't do anything because I'm afraid or else I would have already killed the king, that bloody villain! That remorseless, treacherous villain. I want vengeance! I am such an ass! I, the son of a dear murdered father, with all rights to seek revenge, stand around and do nothing! I need to get control! I have heard that some people are so driven by watching a play they confess their sins out loud. I know! I'll have the players put on a play similar to the murder of my father and I will watch my uncle's reaction. If

And can say nothing; no, not for a king,
Upon whose property and most dear life
A damn'd defeat was made. Am I a coward?
Who calls me villain? breaks my pate across?
Plucks off my beard, and blows it in my face?
Tweaks me by the nose? gives me the lie i' the throat,
As deep as to the lungs? who does me this?
Ha!
'Swounds, I should take it: for it cannot be
But I am pigeon-liver'd and lack gall
To make oppression bitter, or ere this
I should have fatted all the region kites
With this slave's offal: bloody, bawdy villain!
Remorseless, treacherous, lecherous, kindless villain!
O, vengeance!
Why, what an ass am I! This is most brave,
That I, the son of a dear father murder'd,
Prompted to my revenge by heaven and hell,
Must, like a whore, unpack my heart with words,
And fall a-cursing, like a very drab,
A scullion!
Fie upon't! foh! About, my brain! I have heard
That guilty creatures sitting at a play
Have by the very cunning of the scene
Been struck so to the soul that presently
They have proclaim'd their malefactions;
For murder, though it have no tongue, will speak
With most miraculous organ. I'll have these players
Play something like the murder of my father
Before mine uncle: I'll observe his looks;
I'll tent him to the quick: if he but blench,
I know my course. The spirit that I have seen
May be the devil: and the devil hath power
To assume a pleasing shape; yea, and perhaps
Out of my weakness and my melancholy,
As he is very potent with such spirits,
Abuses me to damn me: I'll have grounds
More relative than this: the play 's the thing
Wherein I'll catch the conscience of the king.

Exit

he flinches or becomes pale I will know for sure what to do
because all I have to go on are the words of a ghost. If the ghost
is the devil who is trying to condemn my soul, I need to be
careful before I act. The play will reveal the true conscience of

So his plan it to Show his revenge through the play

Act III

Scene I

A room in the castle

Enter KING CLAUDIUS, QUEEN GERTRUDE, POLONIUS, OPHELIA, ROSENCRANTZ, and GUILDENSTERN

KING CLAUDIUS
And can you, by no drift of circumstance,
Get from him why he puts on this confusion,
Grating so harshly all his days of quiet
With turbulent and dangerous lunacy?

Have you figured out why he is acting so crazy?

ROSENCRANTZ
He does confess he feels himself distracted;
But from what cause he will by no means speak.

He does say he feels distracted, but he did not explain the cause.

GUILDENSTERN
Nor do we find him forward to be sounded,
But, with a crafty madness, keeps aloof,
When we would bring him on to some confession
Of his true state.

He doesn't seem to want to be questioned. He skirts around the issue of how he feels.

QUEEN GERTRUDE
Did he receive you well?

Did he treat you well?

ROSENCRANTZ
Most like a gentleman.

Yes, he was a gentleman.

GUILDENSTERN
But with much forcing of his disposition.

But, it seemed forced, like he had to try to be nice.

ROSENCRANTZ
Niggard of question; but, of our demands,
Most free in his reply.

He didn't ask us any questions, but he answered all of ours.

QUEEN GERTRUDE
Did you assay him?
To any pastime?

Did you ask him to hang out with you?

ROSENCRANTZ
Madam, it so fell out, that certain players
We o'er-raught on the way: of these we told him;
And there did seem in him a kind of joy
To hear of it: they are about the court,
And, as I think, they have already order
This night to play before him.

Madam, it just so happened that a group of actors we knew came up, and when we told Hamlet about them, it seemed to cheer him up. They are supposed to play for him tonight.

LORD POLONIUS
'Tis most true:
And he beseech'd me to entreat your majesties
To hear and see the matter.

It's true, and he asked me to ask you, your majesties, to come and join him.

KING CLAUDIUS
With all my heart; and it doth much content me
To hear him so inclined.
Good gentlemen, give him a further edge,
And drive his purpose on to these delights.

This does my heart good to hear he is interested in something. Gentlemen, please encourage him to attend the play, and maybe it will make him happier.

[Handwritten annotations: "Why ishe acting weird", "he was very welcoming", "very open to answering questions", "wants the royals to see the play"]

ROSENCRANTZ
We shall, my lord.

Exeunt ROSENCRANTZ and GUILDENSTERN

KING CLAUDIUS
Sweet Gertrude, leave us too;
For we have closely sent for Hamlet hither,
That he, as 'twere by accident, may here
Affront Ophelia:
Her father and myself, lawful espials,
Will so bestow ourselves that, seeing, unseen,
We may of their encounter frankly judge,
And gather by him, as he is behaved,
If 't be the affliction of his love or no
That thus he suffers for.

QUEEN GERTRUDE
I shall obey you.
And for your part, Ophelia, I do wish
That your good beauties be the happy cause
Of Hamlet's wildness: so shall I hope your virtues
Will bring him to his wonted way again,
To both your honours.

OPHELIA
Madam, I wish it may.

Exit QUEEN GERTRUDE

LORD POLONIUS
Ophelia, walk you here. Gracious, so please you,
We will bestow ourselves.

To OPHELIA

Read on this book;
Read on this book;
That show of such an exercise may colour
Your loneliness. We are oft to blame in this,--
'Tis too much proved--that with devotion's visage
And pious action we do sugar o'er
The devil himself.

KING CLAUDIUS
[Aside]
O, 'tis too true!
How smart a lash that speech doth give my conscience!
The harlot's cheek, beautied with plastering art,
Is not more ugly to the thing that helps it
Than is my deed to my most painted word:
O heavy burthen!

LORD POLONIUS
I hear him coming: let's withdraw, my lord.

Exeunt KING CLAUDIUS and POLONIUS

Enter HAMLET

HAMLET
To be, or not to be: that is the question:
Whether 'tis nobler in the mind to suffer
The slings and arrows of outrageous fortune,
Or to take arms against a sea of troubles,
And by opposing end them? To die: to sleep;

Handwritten notes: he tells the Queen what the plan is

Handwritten note: Ophelia is well aware of the plan

Handwritten note: he feels attacked by the words

Handwritten note: To live or to die

We will, my lord.

Sweet Gertrude, please leave us alone a minute. We have sent for Hamlet to come here so he may bump into Ophelia. Her father and I are acting as spies. We are trying to see if it is love that is making him act so strangely.

Yes, I'll go. As for you, Ophelia, I do hope it is his infatuation with your beauty that makes him crazy. I also hope your virtue will help him return to his normal state, for both your sakes.

Madam, I wish it, too.

Ophelia, walk over here. We will hide over there.

Read this book and act as if you are alone, like people who act righteous to cover up their evil ways.

That's true!
His words are like daggers to my conscience! The harlot's cheek, covered with makeup is as ugly as the actions I am trying to hide with pretty words. Oh, my heavy heart!

I hear him coming: Let's hide, my lord.

To live or to die...That is the question.
Is it more courageous to suffer through life's horrors or to fight them and perhaps end them? Should I die or like death, sleep, and perhaps dream? Now there's the problem. By sleeping, I would put an end to the torment life offers. Why should anyone

No more; and by a sleep to say we end
The heart-ache and the thousand natural shocks
That flesh is heir to, 'tis a consummation
Devoutly to be wish'd. To die, to sleep;
To sleep: perchance to dream: ay, there's the rub;
For in that sleep of death what dreams may come
When we have shuffled off this mortal coil,
Must give us pause: there's the respect
That makes calamity of so long life;
For who would bear the whips and scorns of time,
The oppressor's wrong, the proud man's contumely,
The pangs of despised love, the law's delay,
The insolence of office and the spurns
That patient merit of the unworthy takes,
When he himself might his quietus make
With a bare bodkin? who would fardels bear,
To grunt and sweat under a weary life,
But that the dread of something after death,
The undiscover'd country from whose bourn
No traveller returns, puzzles the will
And makes us rather bear those ills we have
Than fly to others that we know not of?
Thus conscience does make cowards of us all;
And thus the native hue of resolution
Is sicklied o'er with the pale cast of thought,
And enterprises of great pith and moment
With this regard their currents turn awry,
And lose the name of action.--Soft you now!
The fair Ophelia! Nymph, in thy orisons
Be all my sins remember'd.

choose to live when you must suffer the hands of time, the evil of men, the pain of unreturned love, or the unjust government? Who would endure such struggles in life, but those that dread the unknown of death, the undiscovered country from where travelers never return. Our fear of death makes us all cowards, and we consider our choices too much, keeping us from acting at all. But, wait! The beautiful Ophelia!—Angel, do pray for me.

[handwritten: In this monologue he questions the purpose of life itself]

OPHELIA
Good my lord,
How does your honour for this many a day?

Oh, hello, my lord. How have you been doing?

HAMLET
I humbly thank you; well, well, well.

Very well, thank you.

OPHELIA
My lord, I have remembrances of yours,
That I have longed long to re-deliver;
I pray you, now receive them.

My lord, I have some things that belong to you that I have been wanting to return. Please take them.

HAMLET
No, not I;
I never gave you aught.

[handwritten: Does not want anything]

No, it's not mine. I never gave you anything.

OPHELIA
My honour'd lord, you know right well you did;
And, with them, words of so sweet breath composed
As made the things more rich: their perfume lost,
Take these again; for to the noble mind
Rich gifts wax poor when givers prove unkind.
There, my lord.

My lord, you know very well you did. You gave me the sweetest letters, but they mean nothing to me now. Here they are.

HAMLET
Ha, ha! are you honest?

Ha, ha! Are you telling the truth?

OPHELIA
My lord?

[handwritten: returns the letters from Hamlet]

What?

HAMLET
Are you fair?

OPHELIA
What means your lordship?

HAMLET
That if you be honest and fair, your honesty should admit no discourse to your beauty.

OPHELIA
Could beauty, my lord, have better commerce than with honesty?

HAMLET
Ay, truly; for the power of beauty will sooner transform honesty from what it is to a bawd than the force of honesty can translate beauty into his likeness: this was sometime a paradox, but now the time gives it proof. I did love you once.

OPHELIA
Indeed, my lord, you made me believe so.

HAMLET
You should not have believed me; for virtue cannot so inoculate our old stock but we shall relish of it: I loved you not.

OPHELIA
I was the more deceived.

HAMLET
Get thee to a nunnery: why wouldst thou be a breeder of sinners? I am myself indifferent honest; but yet I could accuse me of such things that it were better my mother had not borne me: I am very proud, revengeful, ambitious, with more offences at my beck than I have thoughts to put them in, imagination to give them shape, or time to act them in. What should such fellows as I do crawling between earth and heaven? We are arrant knaves, all; believe none of us. Go thy ways to a nunnery. Where's your father?

OPHELIA
At home, my lord.

HAMLET
Let the doors be shut upon him, that he may play the fool no where but in's own house. Farewell.

OPHELIA
O, help him, you sweet heavens!

HAMLET
If thou dost marry, I'll give thee this plague for thy dowry: be thou as chaste as ice, as pure as snow, thou shalt not escape calumny. Get thee to a nunnery, go: farewell. Or, if thou wilt needs marry, marry a fool; for wise men know well enough what monsters you make of them. To a nunnery, go,

Are you beautiful?

What are you talking about?

I am saying, if you are honest and beautiful, then your honesty should not affect your beauty.

Is beauty, my lord, more important than honesty?

Yes, because beauty can change a person, but honesty cannot change anything. I used to be confused by this, but I understand now. I used to love you.

You made me think you did.

You should not have believed me, because we are all evil beings. I did not love you.

I was fooled.

Get to a convent or would you rather be a mother to more sinners? I am an honest person, but even I am guilty of sin and it would have been better if I had never been born. I am proud, vengeful, and ambitious, with more sin in my heart than I have time to put into thoughts or actions. What should a man, like me, do? We are all sinners; don't believe any of us. Go find a convent. Where's your father?

At home, my lord.

May he stay there and pretend to be a fool. Goodbye.

O, help him, Lord!

If you do marry, I'll give you this curse as a gift,--Be as cold as ice, pure as snow, but you will not escape trouble. Now, go to a convent. Goodbye. Or, if you need to marry, marry a fool. Smart men know what women will do. Go to a convent, and go quickly. Goodbye.

[Handwritten annotations:]
Is beauty more important to you?

So it was all a trick?

does not see a point in living

Sort of going against her

father

and quickly too. Farewell.

OPHELIA
O heavenly powers, restore him!

Oh God, help him!

HAMLET
I have heard of your paintings too, well enough; God has given you one face, and you make yourselves another: you jig, you amble, and you lisp, and nick-name God's creatures, and make your wantonness your ignorance. Go to, I'll no more on't; it hath made me mad. I say, we will have no more marriages: those that are married already, all but one, shall live; the rest shall keep as they are. To a nunnery, go.

I have heard of how you put on makeup and dance and walk about talking like high society. I have heard of your loose ways. It's driven me crazy. Go on. I declare there will be no more marriages: those that already are married may stay that way, but there will be no more. Take yourself to a convent.

Exit

OPHELIA

O, what a noble mind is here o'erthrown!
The courtier's, soldier's, scholar's, eye, tongue, sword;
The expectancy and rose of the fair state,
The glass of fashion and the mould of form,
The observed of all observers, quite, quite down!
And I, of ladies most deject and wretched,
That suck'd the honey of his music vows,
Now see that noble and most sovereign reason,
Like sweet bells jangled, out of tune and harsh;
That unmatch'd form and feature of blown youth
Blasted with ecstasy: O, woe is me,
To have seen what I have seen, see what I see!

Oh, what a wonderful mind has been lost! He was such a gentleman, a scholar, and soldier. He used to be the pride of the state with his perfect charm and sense of taste. Everyone loved him, wanted to be like him! Now he is so low! And I, of all the ladies who loved to hear his voice, have seen him at his worst. His youthfulness has been killed by madness. Oh, how terrible to see what I have seen, to see what I see, now.

Re-enter KING CLAUDIUS and POLONIUS

KING CLAUDIUS
Love! his affections do not that way tend;
Nor what he spake, though it lack'd form a little,
Was not like madness. There's something in his soul,
O'er which his melancholy sits on brood;
And I do doubt the hatch and the disclose
Will be some danger: which for to prevent,
I have in quick determination
Thus set it down: he shall with speed to England,
For the demand of our neglected tribute
Haply the seas and countries different
With variable objects shall expel
This something-settled matter in his heart,
Whereon his brains still beating puts him thus
From fashion of himself. What think you on't?

Oh, what a wonderful mind has been lost! He was such a gentleman, a scholar, and soldier. He used to be the pride of the state with his perfect charm and sense of taste. Everyone loved him, wanted to be like him! Now he is so low! And I, of all the ladies who loved to hear his voice, have seen him at his worst. His youthfulness has been killed by madness. Oh, how terrible to see what I have seen, to see what I see, now.

LORD POLONIUS
It shall do well: but yet do I believe
The origin and commencement of his grief
Sprung from neglected love. How now, Ophelia!
You need not tell us what Lord Hamlet said;
We heard it all. My lord, do as you please;
But, if you hold it fit, after the play
Let his queen mother all alone entreat him
To show his grief: let her be round with him;

It may work, but I still believe his behavior was caused by his unreturned love for Ophelia. Hello, Ophelia. We heard what Hamlet said. My lord, do whatever pleases you, but if you don't mind, let his mother talk with him alone tonight after the play to see if she can find out what is bothering him. I'll listen to what they say. If she can't get it out of him, then send him to England or wherever you think is best.

[Handwritten annotations: "Now he hates the concept of marriage"; "his joy was ripped out of him"; "he used to be such a bright person"; "love does affect people"]

And I'll be placed, so please you, in the ear
Of all their conference. If she find him not,
To England send him, or confine him where
Your wisdom best shall think.

KING CLAUDIUS
It shall be so:
Madness in great ones must not unwatch'd go.

Okay. We must be watchful of insanity among great men.

Exeunt

Shakespeare shows negative affects of men in power going mad

Scene II

A hall in the castle

Enter HAMLET and Players

HAMLET

Speak the speech, I pray you, as I pronounced it to
you, trippingly on the tongue: but if you mouth it,
as many of your players do, I had as lief the
town-crier spoke my lines. Nor do not saw the air
too much with your hand, thus, but use all gently;
for in the very torrent, tempest, and, as I may say,
the whirlwind of passion, you must acquire and beget
a temperance that may give it smoothness. O, I
offends me to the soul to hear a robustious
periwig-pated fellow tear a passion to tatters, to
very rags, to split the ears of the groundlings, who
for the most part are capable of nothing but
inexplicable dumbshows and noise: I would have such
a fellow whipped for o'erdoing Termagant; it
out-herods Herod: pray you, avoid it.

*Please say the speech like I told you, smoothly and flowingly. If
you start saying it like the other players do, I might as well have
the town crier do it. Don't use your hands too much, either. You
must not get too emotional, because nothing bothers me more
than to hear a fellow in a wig ruin a passionate story with loud,
showy actions to please to the crowd. I would rather whip a man
for performing like the old plays where King Herod went on and
on. Please avoid doing that.*

[handwritten: asking the actors to present the speech]

First Player

I warrant your honour.

I will try, your honor.

HAMLET

Be not too tame neither, but let your own discretion
be your tutor: suit the action to the word, the
word to the action; with this special o'erstep not
the modesty of nature: for any thing so overdone is
from the purpose of playing, whose end, both at the
first and now, was and is, to hold, as 'twere, the
mirror up to nature; to show virtue her own feature,
scorn her own image, and the very age and body of
the time his form and pressure. Now this overdone,
or come tardy off, though it make the unskilful
laugh, cannot but make the judicious grieve; the
censure of the which one must in your allowance
o'erweigh a whole theatre of others. O, there be
players that I have seen play, and heard others
praise, and that highly, not to speak it profanely,
that, neither having the accent of Christians nor
the gait of Christian, pagan, nor man, have so
strutted and bellowed that I have thought some of
nature's journeymen had made men and not made them
well, they imitated humanity so abominably.

*Don't be too tame, either. Use your instincts. Make sure the
action suits the word and vice-versa. Just be natural and don't
overdo it. I want this play to be believable. Don't perform just to
make the commoners laugh, while the other listeners must suffer.
I have seen plays performed like that, and I couldn't stand it; the
performers were so inept.*

[handwritten: wants it to look very natural and genuine]

[handwritten: → wants a good show]

First Player

I hope we have reformed that indifferently with us, sir.

I hope we please you, sir.

HAMLET

O, reform it altogether. And let those that play
your clowns speak no more than is set down for them;
for there be of them that will themselves laugh, to
set on some quantity of barren spectators to laugh
too; though, in the mean time, some necessary
question of the play be then to be considered:

*I'm sure you will. And don't let your comedians improvise and
ruin the play. Only amateurs attempt to win over the audience
with vile humor. Go get ready.*

[handwritten: ↳ stick to the script]

that's villanous, and shows a most pitiful ambition
in the fool that uses it. Go, make you ready.

Exeunt Players

Enter POLONIUS, ROSENCRANTZ, and GUILDENSTERN

How now, my lord! I will the king hear this piece of work?   *Hello, my lord! Is the king attending the play?*

LORD POLONIUS
And the queen too, and that presently.   *The queen is coming, too. They should be here soon.*

HAMLET
Bid the players make haste.   *Tell the actors to hurry.*

both monarchs will be attending

Exit POLONIUS

Will you two help to hasten them?   *Will you two go hurry them along?*

ROSENCRANTZ GUILDENSTERN
We will, my lord.   *We will, my lord.*

Exeunt ROSENCRANTZ and GUILDENSTERN

HAMLET
What ho! Horatio!   *Hey, Horatio? What's up?*

Enter HORATIO

HORATIO
Here, sweet lord, at your service.   *I am here to serve you, lord.*

HAMLET
Horatio, thou art e'en as just a man   *You are just the man with whom I need to speak.*
As e'er my conversation coped withal.

Still trusts him

HORATIO
O, my dear lord,--   *O, my lord,--*

HAMLET
Nay, do not think I flatter;   *I'm not trying to flatter you. I don't want anything. I am being*
For what advancement may I hope from thee   *sincere. A play is being held tonight resembling the situation of*
That no revenue hast but thy good spirits,   *which you are aware. When the similar scene takes place, look*
To feed and clothe thee? Why should the poor be flatter'd?   *at my uncle. If he does not look guilty, then I will know the ghost*
No, let the candied tongue lick absurd pomp,   *was a fake and I am a fool. I will be looking, too. Afterwards, we*
And crook the pregnant hinges of the knee   *will compare what we saw.*
Where thrift may follow fawning. Dost thou hear?
Since my dear soul was mistress of her choice
And could of men distinguish, her election
Hath seal'd thee for herself; for thou hast been
As one, in suffering all, that suffers nothing,
A man that fortune's buffets and rewards
Hast ta'en with equal thanks: and blest are those
Whose blood and judgment are so well commingled,
That they are not a pipe for fortune's finger
To sound what stop she please. Give me that man
That is not passion's slave, and I will wear him
In my heart's core, ay, in my heart of heart,
As I do thee.--Something too much of this.--
There is a play to night before the king;
One scene of it comes near the circumstance

wants to show his sincerity and revenge through the play

63

Which I have told thee of my father's death:
I prithee, when thou seest that act afoot,
Even with the very comment of thy soul
Observe mine uncle: if his occulted guilt   → wants claudius
Do not itself unkennel in one speech,   to feel guilty
It is a damned ghost that we have seen,
And my imaginations are as foul
As Vulcan's stithy. Give him heedful note;
For I mine eyes will rivet to his face,
And after we will both our judgments join
In censure of his seeming.

HORATIO
Well, my lord: *I will watch him, my lord. His reaction will not escape me.*
If he steal aught the whilst this play is playing,
And 'scape detecting, I will pay the theft.

HAMLET
They are coming to the play; I must be idle: *Here they come. I have to look normal. Go get a seat.*
Get you a place.   act natural

Danish march. A flourish. Enter KING CLAUDIUS, QUEEN GERTRUDE, POLONIUS, OPHELIA, ROSENCRANTZ,
GUILDENSTERN, and others

KING CLAUDIUS
How fares our cousin Hamlet?   *How is our cousin Hamlet?*

HAMLET
Excellent, i' faith; of the chameleon's dish: I eat   *I am as excellent as can be. I eat the air like the chameleons.*
the air, promise-crammed: you cannot feed capons so.

KING CLAUDIUS
I have nothing with this answer, Hamlet; these words   *I don't know what to say, Hamlet. I don't understand you.*
are not mine.

HAMLET   Says he
No, nor mine now.   is doing   *Me either.*
                                                              well
To POLONIUS

My lord, you played once i' the university, you say?   *My lord, didn't you perform once at the university?*

LORD POLONIUS
That did I, my lord; and was accounted a good actor.   *Yes I did, my lord, and I was pretty good.*

HAMLET
What did you enact?   *What play did you perform?*

LORD POLONIUS
I did enact Julius Caesar: I was killed i' the   *I was in Julius Caesar. I was killed in the Capitol by Brutus.*
Capitol; Brutus killed me.
                                          Allusion
HAMLET
It was a brute part of him to kill so capital a calf   *What a brute to slaughter such a capital calf.*
there. Be the players ready?   *Are the performers ready?*

ROSENCRANTZ
Ay, my lord; they stay upon your patience. making   *Yes, sir, they are waiting for you.*
                                            awareness
QUEEN GERTRUDE   of
Come hither, my dear Hamlet, sit by me.   murder   *Come here, Hamlet, and sit by me.*

64

HAMLET
No, good mother, here's metal more attractive.
LORD POLONIUS
[To KING CLAUDIUS]
O, ho! do you mark that?

they are getting more suhpicious

HAMLET
Lady, shall I lie in your lap?

Lying down at OPHELIA's feet

OPHELIA
No, my lord.

HAMLET
I mean, my head upon your lap?

OPHELIA
Ay, my lord.

HAMLET
Do you think I meant country matters?

OPHELIA
I think nothing, my lord.

HAMLET
That's a fair thought to lie between maids' legs.

that is a very strange line

OPHELIA
What is, my lord?

HAMLET
Nothing.

OPHELIA
You are merry, my lord.

HAMLET
Who, I?

OPHELIA
Ay, my lord.

HAMLET
O God, your only jig-maker. What should a man do
but be merry? for, look you, how cheerfully my
mother looks, and my father died within these two hours.

OPHELIA
Nay, 'tis twice two months, my lord.

Still reflecting on the death. and wedding

HAMLET
So long? Nay then, let the devil wear black, for
I'll have a suit of sables. O heavens! die two
months ago, and not forgotten yet? Then there's
hope a great man's memory may outlive his life half
a year: but, by'r lady, he must build churches,
then; or else shall he suffer not thinking on, with
the hobby-horse, whose epitaph is 'For, O, for, O,

No, Mother, this seat is better.

Did you hear that? What do you make of it?

Lady, may I lie in your lap?

No, my lord.

I mean with my head in your lap.

Yes, my lord.

Did you think I meant something inappropriate?

I wasn't thinking anything, my lord.

That's a nice thought to lie between a girl's legs.

What is, sir?

Nothing.

You are happy, my lord.

Who, me?

Yes, my lord.

Oh, you silly girl! What man wouldn't be happy? Just look at my mother, how happy she looks, with my father only dead a couple of hours.

It's been over four months, my lord.

That long? Well then, for whom am I mourning? Oh God! Dead two months, and not quite forgotten. There is hope for a man's memory, that it may outlive him. But, he's got to build churches for that to happen. Otherwise, he will be like the carnival, soon forgotten.

the hobby-horse is forgot.'

Hautboys play. The dumb-show *enters*
Enter a King and a Queen very lovingly; the Queen embracing him, and he her. She kneels, and makes show of protestation unto him. He takes her up, and declines his head upon her neck: lays him down upon a bank of flowers: she, seeing him asleep, leaves him. Anon comes in a fellow, takes off his crown, kisses it, and pours poison in the King's ears, and exit. The Queen returns; finds the King dead, and makes passionate action. The Poisoner, with some two or three Mutes, comes in again, seeming to lament with her. The dead body is carried away. The Poisoner wooes the Queen with gifts: she seems loath and unwilling awhile, but in the end accepts his love

Exeunt

OPHELIA
What means this, my lord?

What do you mean, my lord?

HAMLET
Marry, this is miching mallecho; it means mischief.

It means mischief is brewing.

[handwritten: Is he proud?]

OPHELIA
Belike this show imports the argument of the play.

The play is about to begin.

Enter Prologue

HAMLET
We shall know by this fellow: the players cannot
keep counsel; they'll tell all.

Here comes the players. They are about to begin.

OPHELIA
Will he tell us what this show meant?

Will he give us an introduction?

HAMLET
Ay, or any show that you'll show him: be not you
ashamed to show, he'll not shame to tell you what it means.

Yes, or you can put a play on for him. Don't be ashamed to play and let him tell the story.

OPHELIA
You are naught, you are naught: I'll mark the play.

You are naughty. I'll watch the actors.

Prologue
For us, and for our tragedy,
Here stooping to your clemency,
We beg your hearing patiently.

[handwritten: Intends on watching the play]

We humbly present our tragedy for your enjoyment. Please listen.

Exit

HAMLET
Is this a prologue, or the posy of a ring?

Was that the prologue or an inscription on a ring?

OPHELIA
'Tis brief, my lord.

It was brief, my lord.

HAMLET
As woman's love.

[handwritten: As breif as a womens love, targetted]

As a woman's love.

Enter two Players, King and Queen

Player King
Full thirty times hath Phoebus' cart gone round
Neptune's salt wash and Tellus' orbed ground,
And thirty dozen moons with borrow'd sheen
About the world have times twelve thirties been,

We have been married now for thirty years.

Since love our hearts and Hymen did our hands
Unite commutual in most sacred bands.

Player Queen
So many journeys may the sun and moon
Make us again count o'er ere love be done!
But, woe is me, you are so sick of late,
So far from cheer and from your former state,
That I distrust you. Yet, though I distrust,
Discomfort you, my lord, it nothing must:
For women's fear and love holds quantity;
In neither aught, or in extremity.
Now, what my love is, proof hath made you know;
And as my love is sized, my fear is so:
Where love is great, the littlest doubts are fear;
Where little fears grow great, great love grows there.

I hope we have thirty more, but you have not been yourself lately. You seem sad. But, I am just a woman who fears the loss of her love.

the queen actors fears loving her lover

Player King
'Faith, I must leave thee, love, and shortly too;
My operant powers their functions leave to do:
And thou shalt live in this fair world behind,
Honour'd, beloved; and haply one as kind
For husband shalt thou--

I am afraid I must leave you soon. My body is old and does not work like it used to. You will probably find another husband.

Player Queen
O, confound the rest!
Such love must needs be treason in my breast:
Such love must needs be treason in my breast:
In second husband let me be accurst!
None wed the second but who kill'd the first.

No man compares to you. I would rather be cursed than to marry again. When a woman marries a second time, she surely

HAMLET
[Aside]
Wormwood, wormwood.

death is better than re-marriage

Ouch!

Player Queen
The instances that second marriage move
Are base respects of thrift, but none of love:
A second time I kill my husband dead,
When second husband kisses me in bed.

A second marriage may be for money, but not for love. If I were to kiss my second husband, it would be like killing my first all over again.

Player King
I do believe you think what now you speak;
But what we do determine oft we break.
Purpose is but the slave to memory,
Of violent birth, but poor validity;
Which now, like fruit unripe, sticks on the tree;
But fall, unshaken, when they mellow be.
Most necessary 'tis that we forget
To pay ourselves what to ourselves is debt:
What to ourselves in passion we propose,
The passion ending, doth the purpose lose.
The violence of either grief or joy
Their own enactures with themselves destroy:
Where joy most revels, grief doth most lament;
Grief joys, joy grieves, on slender accident.
This world is not for aye, nor 'tis not strange
That even our loves should with our fortunes change;
For 'tis a question left us yet to prove,
Whether love lead fortune, or else fortune love.
The great man down, you mark his favourite flies;

I know you believe what you are saying, now, but, you may change your mind. What we promise ourselves during times of great emotion, we may not keep when the emotions subside. After I am gone, your love and grief will run its course and then you may remarry.

Saying what actually happened in the life of Hamlet

The poor advanced makes friends of enemies.
And hitherto doth love on fortune tend;
For who not needs shall never lack a friend,
And who in want a hollow friend doth try,
Directly seasons him his enemy.
But, orderly to end where I begun,
Our wills and fates do so contrary run
That our devices still are overthrown;
Our thoughts are ours, their ends none of our own:
So think thou wilt no second husband wed;
But die thy thoughts when thy first lord is dead.

Player Queen
Nor earth to me give food, nor heaven light!
Sport and repose lock from me day and night!
To desperation turn my trust and hope!
An anchor's cheer in prison be my scope!
Each opposite that blanks the face of joy
Meet what I would have well and it destroy!
Both here and hence pursue me lasting strife,
If, once a widow, ever I be wife!

I will starve first! I will lock myself away in prison before I remarry. I will be a widow forever.

HAMLET
If she should break it now!

She will break that vow!

Contradicts the message of love

Player King
'Tis deeply sworn. Sweet, leave me here awhile;
My spirits grow dull, and fain I would beguile
The tedious day with sleep.

You have sworn with great passion. Leave me for awhile. I would like to take a nap.

Sleeps

Player Queen
Sleep rock thy brain,
And never come mischance between us twain!

Sleep tight and let nothing ever come between us!

Exit

HAMLET
Madam, how like you this play?

Madam, how are you liking this play?

QUEEN GERTRUDE
The lady protests too much, methinks.

I think the lady is overplaying it.

HAMLET
O, but she'll keep her word. *does not see the connection*

Oh, but she'll keep her word.

KING CLAUDIUS
Have you heard the argument? Is there no offence in 't?

Have you seen this play before? Is there anything offensive in it?

HAMLET
No, no, they do but jest, poison in jest; no offence
i' the world.

No, no! It's just a joke. I don't think it is offensive at all.

KING CLAUDIUS
What do you call the play?

What is the name of the play?

HAMLET *clever*
The Mouse-trap. Marry, how? Tropically. This play
is the image of a murder done in Vienna: Gonzago is
the duke's name; his wife, Baptista: you shall see

The Mouse-trap. Why? The play is about a murder in Vienna. Gonzago is the duke and his wife is Baptista. You will see, it's just a common play. It might be uncomfortable for some, but we

anon; 'tis a knavish piece of work: but what o'
that? your majesty and we that have free souls, it
touches us not:
let the galled jade wince, our withers are unwrung.

are guilt-free, so we can watch it without it bothering us.

no guilt in the play

Enter LUCIANUS

This is one Lucianus, nephew to the king.

This is Lucianus, the king's nephew.

OPHELIA
You are as good as a chorus, my lord.

You are a good interpreter, my lord.

HAMLET
I could interpret between you and your love, if I
could see the puppets dallying.

I could even interpret your relationship with your lover, if ever I saw you together.

OPHELIA
You are keen, my lord, you are keen.

You're so smart, my lord, so smart.

HAMLET
It would cost you a groaning to take off my edge.

You could make me relax, but it may make you groan a little.

OPHELIA
Still better, and worse.

You are so funny! Not!

In a sexual manner?

HAMLET
So you must take your husbands. Begin, murderer;
pox, leave thy damnable faces, and begin. Come:
'the croaking raven doth bellow for revenge.'

That's what women get when they get married.—But, let the murdering begin. Hurry up! "The croaking raven doth bellow for revenge."

LUCIANUS
Thoughts black, hands apt, drugs fit, and time agreeing;
Confederate season, else no creature seeing;
Thou mixture rank, of midnight weeds collected,
With Hecate's ban thrice blasted, thrice infected,
Thy natural magic and dire property,
On wholesome life usurp immediately.

I am ready. My thoughts are dark, my hands are still, the drugs are here, and it is time. The darkness obscures my actions. Let the magic do its work and take life quickly.

Pours the poison into the sleeper's ears

his dark thoughts take him over

HAMLET
He poisons him i' the garden for's estate.
His name's Gonzago: the story is extant, and writ in
choice Italian: you shall see anon how the murderer
gets the love of Gonzago's wife.

He poisons him in the estates' garden. His name's Gonzago. The story is in the finest Italian. Now, you will see how the murderer seduces the duke's wife.

OPHELIA
The king rises.

The King is getting up.

HAMLET
What, frighted with false fire!

What? Is he scared of this pretend play?

QUEEN GERTRUDE
How fares my lord?

Are you feeling okay, my lord?

LORD POLONIUS
Give o'er the play.

Stop the play.

KING CLAUDIUS
Give me some light; away!

Someone turn on the lights. I've got to get out of here!

suddenly has an urge to leave

All
Lights, lights, lights!

Lights! Lights!

Exeunt all but HAMLET and HORATIO

HAMLET
Why, let the stricken deer go weep,
The hart ungalled play;
For some must watch, while some must sleep:
So runs the world away.
Would not this, sir, and a forest of feathers-- if
the rest of my fortunes turn Turk with me--with two
Provincial roses on my razed shoes, get me a
fellowship in a cry of players, sir?

Oh, let the hunted deer go weep, and let everyone else watch the play. I am putting up such a fine act, I may have to become an actor one day.

(handwritten: he got his message across)

HORATIO
Half a share.

They might pay you half of the profits.

HAMLET
A whole one, I.
For thou dost know, O Damon dear,
This realm dismantled was
Of Jove himself; and now reigns here
A very, very--pajock.

I want all of it.
For you know, my dear friend.
This realm was rid of God, himself. And now reigns a peacock.

(handwritten: wants the entire profit)

HORATIO
You might have rhymed.

You might have rhymed.

HAMLET
O good Horatio, I'll take the ghost's word for a
thousand pound. Didst perceive?

Oh Horatio, I'll take the ghost's word for the truth. What did you think?

HORATIO
Very well, my lord.

I agree, my lord.

(handwritten: he believes the ghost)

HAMLET
Upon the talk of the poisoning?

Did you see how he acted when they mentioned poison?

HORATIO
I did very well note him.

I did, sir.

HAMLET
Ah, ha! Come, some music! come, the recorders!
For if the king like not the comedy,
Why then, belike, he likes it not, perdy.
Come, some music!

Ah ha! Let's have some music. Let the musicians play their instruments! If the king doesn't like the comedy, oh well! Come on, music!

Re-enter ROSENCRANTZ and GUILDENSTERN

(handwritten: losing interest in what the king likes)

GUILDENSTERN
Good my lord, vouchsafe me a word with you.

My lord, could I have a word with you?

HAMLET
Sir, a whole history.

You can have many words, a whole history.

GUILDENSTERN
The king, sir,--

Well, the king, sir...

HAMLET
Ay, sir, what of him?

Yes, what of him?

GUILDENSTERN
Is in his retirement marvellous distempered.

He is resting and he is very upset.

HAMLET
With drink, sir?

Is he drunk, sir?

GUILDENSTERN
No, my lord, rather with choler.

Very angry King

No, my lord, he is angry.

HAMLET
Your wisdom should show itself more richer to
signify this to his doctor; for, for me to put him
to his purgation would perhaps plunge him into far
more choler.

You would be wise to tell his doctor. If I were to help, I would only make him angrier.

GUILDENSTERN
Good my lord, put your discourse into some frame and
start not so wildly from my affair.

Says we cannot help

Please, my lord, try to be sensible.

HAMLET
I am tame, sir: pronounce.

Okay, I'm listening.

GUILDENSTERN
The queen, your mother, in most great affliction of
spirit, hath sent me to you.

The queen, your mother, is very upset and has sent for you.

HAMLET
You are welcome.

the mother is also upset

Glad you could come.

GUILDENSTERN
Nay, good my lord, this courtesy is not of the right
breed. If it shall please you to make me a
wholesome answer, I will do your mother's
commandment: if not, your pardon and my return
shall be the end of my business.

You are not being good, my lord. If you cannot give me an answer, then I will excuse myself and return to your mother.

HAMLET
Sir, I cannot.

Sir, I can't.

GUILDENSTERN
What, my lord?

Can't what, my lord?

HAMLET
Make you a wholesome answer; my wit's diseased: but,
sir, such answer as I can make, you shall command;
or, rather, as you say, my mother: therefore no
more, but to the matter: my mother, you say,--

talks of his messed up mind

I can't give you a good answer because my mind is not right, but, I'll be as honest as possible. So, what did my mother want?

ROSENCRANTZ
Then thus she says; your behavior hath struck her
into amazement and admiration.

She says your behavior has amazed her and she is very proud of you.

HAMLET
O wonderful son, that can so astonish a mother!
But is there no sequel at the heels of this mother's
admiration? Impart.

Oh, what a wonderful son who can fill his mother with pride. But, what does she want?

ROSENCRANTZ
She desires to speak with you in her closet, ere you go
to bed.

I was not expecting this

She wants to speak with you in her room before you go to bed.

71

HAMLET

We shall obey, were she ten times our mother. Have
you any further trade with us?

We shall obey ten times over. Anything else?

ROSENCRANTZ

My lord, you once did love me.

My lord, we were once friends.

[handwritten: feels like they are not friends]

HAMLET

So I do still, by these pickers and stealers.

We still are. I swear by these hands.

ROSENCRANTZ

Good my lord, what is your cause of distemper?
you do, surely, bar the door upon your own liberty, if
you deny your griefs to your friend.

Good, my lord. What is wrong with you?
You can't be a free man with all of your grief locked up inside.

HAMLET

Sir, I lack advancement.

Sir, I can't see any future for myself.

[handwritten: does not know his griefs]

ROSENCRANTZ

How can that be, when you have the voice of the king
himself for your succession in Denmark?

*How is that possible, when you will be the next king of
Denmark?*

HAMLET

Ay, but sir, 'While the grass grows,'--the proverb
is something musty.

*Yes, but how does the old proverb go: 'While the grass grows...'
Oh, that is an old one.*

Re-enter Players with recorders

O, the recorders! let me see one. To withdraw with
you:--why do you go about to recover the wind of me,
as if you would drive me into a toil?

*Oh, the recorders are here. Let me see one. Hey, why are you
standing so close, as if you would like to kill me?*

[handwritten: Is there a murder attempt?]

GUILDENSTERN

O, my lord, if my duty be too bold, my love is too
unmannerly.

Oh, sorry, my lord. I just am concerned about you.

HAMLET

I do not well understand that. Will you play upon
this pipe?

I don't understand why. Here play this.

GUILDENSTERN

My lord, I cannot.

My lord, I can't.

HAMLET

I pray you.

Come on. I am begging.

GUILDENSTERN

Believe me, I cannot.

Believe me, I can't.

HAMLET

I do beseech you.

Please, for me.

GUILDENSTERN

I know no touch of it, my lord.

I don't know how.

HAMLET

[handwritten: they get on Guildenstern playing the recorder]

'Tis as easy as lying: govern these ventages with
your lingers and thumb, give it breath with your
mouth, and it will discourse most eloquent music.
Look you, these are the stops.

*It's as easy as lying. Put your fingers and thumb here and blow.
It will make the most beautiful music. Here are the holes.*

GUILDENSTERN

But these cannot I command to any utterance of harmony; I have not the skill.

I don't have the skill to make music.

HAMLET
Why, look you now, how unworthy a thing you make of me! You would play upon me; you would seem to know my stops; you would pluck out the heart of my mystery; you would sound me from my lowest note to the top of my compass: and there is much music, excellent voice, in this little organ; yet cannot you make it speak. 'Sblood, do you think I am easier to be played on than a pipe? Call me what instrument you will, though you can fret me, yet you cannot play upon me.

Who do you think I am? You try to play me. You seem to know my holes. You wish to know my secrets, and try to search my soul. Yet, you cannot play a single note from this little instrument. How is it you think you can manipulate me, but not this pipe? You will not play me for a fool.

Enter POLONIUS

God bless you, sir!

God bless you, sir!

LORD POLONIUS
My lord, the queen would speak with you, and presently.

My lord, the queen wants to speak with you now.

HAMLET
Do you see yonder cloud that's almost in shape of a camel?

Do you see the cloud over there, shaped like a camel?

LORD POLONIUS
By the mass, and 'tis like a camel, indeed.

I do and it does look like a camel.

HAMLET
Methinks it is like a weasel.

I think it looks more like a weasel.

LORD POLONIUS
It is backed like a weasel.

Its back is like a weasel.

HAMLET
Or like a whale?

Or like a whale?

LORD POLONIUS
Very like a whale.

It is very much like a whale.

HAMLET
Then I will come to my mother by and by. They fool me to the top of my bent. I will come by and by.

Now I will go see my mother, if you will stop messing with me.

LORD POLONIUS
I will say so.

I will tell her.

HAMLET
By and by is easily said.

That is easy to say.

Exit POLONIUS

Leave me, friends.

Please leave me alone.

Exeunt all but HAMLET

Tis now the very witching time of night,
When churchyards yawn and hell itself breathes out
Contagion to this world: now could I drink hot blood,
And do such bitter business as the day
Would quake to look on. Soft! now to my mother.

Now is the time when witches come out, graves open, and hell releases its demons into the world. The time to seek revenge is here. I must go to my mother, but I mustn't lose my nerve. I must be cruel but not murderous. I must speak with bitter words, but not poison her. So, I will be in internal conflict.

[handwritten annotations: "says he cannot"; "he will not be manipulated"; "agreeing with everything Hamlet says"; "revenge has come"]

73

O heart, lose not thy nature; let not ever
The soul of Nero enter this firm bosom:
Let me be cruel, not unnatural:
I will speak daggers to her, but use none;
My tongue and soul in this be hypocrites;
How in my words soever she be shent,
To give them seals never, my soul, consent!

Exit

had no
intention
of murdering
her

Scene III.

A room in the castle

Enter KING CLAUDIUS, ROSENCRANTZ, and GUILDENSTERN

KING CLAUDIUS
I like him not, nor stands it safe with us
To let his madness range. Therefore prepare you;
I your commission will forthwith dispatch,
And he to England shall along with you:
The terms of our estate may not endure
Hazard so dangerous as doth hourly grow
Out of his lunacies.

I don't like the way he's acting and it's not safe for this madness to go on. Therefore, get ready. I'm sending you and Hamlet to England.

[handwritten: Sending Hamlet into exile]

GUILDENSTERN
We will ourselves provide:
Most holy and religious fear it is
To keep those many many bodies safe
That live and feed upon your majesty.

We will gladly do our duty to all the people who depend on your majesty.

ROSENCRANTZ
The single and peculiar life is bound,
With all the strength and armour of the mind,
To keep itself from noyance; but much more
That spirit upon whose weal depend and rest
The lives of many. The cease of majesty
Dies not alone; but, like a gulf, doth draw
What's near it with it: it is a massy wheel,
Fix'd on the summit of the highest mount,
To whose huge spokes ten thousand lesser things
Are mortised and adjoin'd; which, when it falls,
Each small annexment, petty consequence,
Attends the boisterous ruin. Never alone
Did the king sigh, but with a general groan.

Everyone's existence depends on the strength of the mind and thus, requires some protection. But the life of a king, that many lives depend upon, requires far stronger protection. A king is like a wheel on top of a mountain, and when it falls, everything in its path falls, too. When a king feels pain, everyone hurts.

[handwritten: the King needs protection for the greater good]

KING CLAUDIUS
Arm you, I pray you, to this speedy voyage;
For we will fetters put upon this fear,
Which now goes too free-footed.

Please get ready quickly for this trip. We must put an end to this craziness.

ROSENCRANTZ GUILDENSTERN
We will haste us.

We will hurry.

Exeunt ROSENCRANTZ and GUILDENSTERN

Enter POLONIUS

LORD POLONIUS
My lord, he's going to his mother's closet:
Behind the arras I'll convey myself,
To hear the process; and warrant she'll tax him home:
And, as you said, and wisely was it said,
'Tis meet that some more audience than a mother,
Since nature makes them partial, should o'erhear
The speech, of vantage. Fare you well, my liege:
I'll call upon you ere you go to bed,
And tell you what I know.

My lord, he's going to his mother's bedroom. I'll hide behind the curtain and listen. I'll bet she gives him an earful. And, as you wisely said, 'It is better to have someone listen to the conversation other than a mother who may be bias.' I'll come back before you go to bed to tell you what I heard.

[handwritten: Intends on spying on Hamlet]

KING CLAUDIUS
Thanks, dear my lord.
Exit POLONIUS

Thanks, my lord.

O, my offence is rank it smells to heaven;
It hath the primal eldest curse upon't,
A brother's murder. Pray can I not,
Though inclination be as sharp as will:
My stronger guilt defeats my strong intent;
And, like a man to double business bound,
I stand in pause where I shall first begin,
And both neglect. What if this cursed hand
Were thicker than itself with brother's blood,
Is there not rain enough in the sweet heavens
To wash it white as snow? Whereto serves mercy
But to confront the visage of offence?
And what's in prayer but this two-fold force,
To be forestalled ere we come to fall,
Or pardon'd being down? Then I'll look up;
My fault is past. But, O, what form of prayer
Can serve my turn? 'Forgive me my foul murder'?
That cannot be; since I am still possess'd
Of those effects for which I did the murder,
My crown, mine own ambition and my queen.
May one be pardon'd and retain the offence?
In the corrupted currents of this world
Offence's gilded hand may shove by justice,
And oft 'tis seen the wicked prize itself
Buys out the law: but 'tis not so above;
There is no shuffling, there the action lies
In his true nature; and we ourselves compell'd,
Even to the teeth and forehead of our faults,
To give in evidence. What then? what rests?
Try what repentance can: what can it not?
Yet what can it when one can not repent?
O wretched state! O bosom black as death!
O limed soul, that, struggling to be free,
Art more engaged! Help, angels! Make assay!
Bow, stubborn knees; and, heart with strings of steel,
Be soft as sinews of the newborn babe!
All may be well.

Retires and kneels

Enter HAMLET

HAMLET
Now might I do it pat, now he is praying;
And now I'll do't. And so he goes to heaven;
And so am I revenged. That would be scann'd:
A villain kills my father; and for that,
I, his sole son, do this same villain send
To heaven.
O, this is hire and salary, not revenge.
He took my father grossly, full of bread;
With all his crimes broad blown, as flush as May;
And how his audit stands who knows save heaven?
But in our circumstance and course of thought,
'Tis heavy with him: and am I then revenged,
To take him in the purging of his soul,

Oh, my crime is so awful, it smells to high heavens. It has the mark of a brother's murder. I can't pray, even though I want. I am like a man with so much to do, not knowing where to start, I stand still. If this hand is covered in my brother's blood, is there not enough rain to rinse it clean? Isn't this what God's mercy is for? And, isn't this what prayer is for, to protect us from sin and forgiveness? So, I'll pray. I have already sinned. But, what kind of prayer? Forgive me Lord for my horrible crime? That won't work since I am still reaping the rewards of my sin, the crown and the queen. Can one be forgiven and still keep the rewards of sin. What passes in this world does not in heaven. Nothing goes unseen. So what can I do? Maybe I can offer repentance. It couldn't hurt, but it won't help either. My heart is black as death and my soul is full of sin. Help me angels! Come on knees and bend. Heart, be as soft as a newborn, so I can pray.

I could do it easily now; he is praying. He goes to heaven and I have my revenge. The villain who killed my father, I put to death. But, that is too good for him, to kill him when he is ready. He killed my father in the prime of his life without thought to his afterlife, which doesn't appear to be so good. Not now, sword. We will wait until he is drunk or in a rage or in his incestuous bed. Perhaps, we will kill while he is gambling, swearing, or some other sinful act for which there is no forgiveness. Then, we will kill him so his soul may be damned to hell where it belongs. My mother waits for me. Death waits for the king.

[handwritten annotations: "the reader can now confirm that the king really did kill his brother", "he has become vile", "will he kill the king here?"]

76

When he is fit and season'd for his passage?
No!
Up, sword; and know thou a more horrid hent:
When he is drunk asleep, or in his rage,
Or in the incestuous pleasure of his bed;
At gaming, swearing, or about some act
That has no relish of salvation in't;
Then trip him, that his heels may kick at heaven,
And that his soul may be as damn'd and black
As hell, whereto it goes. My mother stays:
This physic but prolongs thy sickly days.

Death awaits the king

Exit

KING CLAUDIUS
[Rising]
My words fly up, my thoughts remain below:
Words without thoughts never to heaven go.

My prayers are just words without meaning. They will never be heard.

Exit

only the worst is coming to him

Scene IV

The Queen's closet

Enter QUEEN GERTRUDE and POLONIUS

LORD POLONIUS
He will come straight. Look you lay home to him:
Tell him his pranks have been too broad to bear with,
And that your grace hath screen'd and stood between
Much heat and him. I'll sconce me even here.
Pray you, be round with him.

He is coming soon. Make sure you give him a good talking to about his pranks. Tell him how you have protected him. I'll be here, but he won't know it. Be firm with him!

his joking must come to an end

HAMLET
[Within]
Mother, mother, mother!

Mother, mother, mother!

QUEEN GERTRUDE
I will, don't worry. Hide, I hear him coming. I'll warrant you,
Fear me not: withdraw, I hear him coming.

I will. Hide, he is coming.

POLONIUS hides behind the arras

Enter HAMLET

HAMLET
Now, mother, what's the matter?

Now, mother, what's the matter?

QUEEN GERTRUDE
Hamlet, thou hast thy father much offended.

Hamlet, you have offended your father.

offended with the truth

HAMLET
Mother, you have my father much offended.

Mother, you are the one who has offended my father

QUEEN GERTRUDE
Come, come, you answer with an idle tongue.

Come now. Talk sensibly.

HAMLET
Go, go, you question with a wicked tongue.

Go on. You are questioning me angrily.

QUEEN GERTRUDE
Why, how now, Hamlet!

What are you talking about, Hamlet?

HAMLET
What's the matter now?

What's the matter now!

QUEEN GERTRUDE
Have you forgot me?

Have you forgotten who I am?

she is his mother

HAMLET
No, by the rood, not so:
You are the queen, your husband's brother's wife;
And--would it were not so!--you are my mother.

Of course not. You are the queen; your husband's brother's wife. And although I wish it were not true, you are my mother.

QUEEN GERTRUDE
Nay, then, I'll set those to you that can speak.
into you.

Alright then, I'll bring in someone who can speak some sense into you.

does not like her

HAMLET
Come, come, and sit you down; you shall not budge;
You go not till I set you up a glass
Where you may see the inmost part of you.

No. Sit down. You will not leave until I give you a mirror and show you your true self.

QUEEN GERTRUDE
What wilt thou do? thou wilt not murder me?
Help, help, ho!

thinks that Hamlet will kill her

What are you going to do? Murder me? Help, help!

LORD POLONIUS
[Behind]
What is going on? Help! Help!
What, ho! help, help, help!

Help! Help!

HAMLET
[Drawing]
What now? A rat? He'll be a dead rat, I bet!
How now! a rat? Dead, for a ducat, dead!

What now?

Makes a pass through the arras

LORD POLONIUS
[Behind]
O, I am slain! ——→ *he killed Ophelias father*

Oh, I am killed!

Falls and dies

QUEEN GERTRUDE
O me, what hast thou done?

Oh no! What have you done?

HAMLET
Nay, I know not:
Is it the king?

I do not know. Is it the king?

QUEEN GERTRUDE
O, what a rash and bloody deed is this!

Oh what a horrible, bloody deed this is!

HAMLET
A bloody deed! almost as bad, good mother,
As kill a king, and marry with his brother.

It is a bloody deed; almost as bad, good mother, as killing a king and marrying his brother.

QUEEN GERTRUDE
As kill a king!

exposing her

As killing a king!

HAMLET
Ay, lady, 'twas my word.

Yes, lady, that's what I said.

Lifts up the array and discovers POLONIUS

Thou wretched, rash, intruding fool, farewell!
I took thee for thy better: take thy fortune;
Thou find'st to be too busy is some danger.
Leave wringing of your hands: peace! sit you down, *calling her stupid*
And let me wring your heart; for so I shall,
If it be made of penetrable stuff,
If damned custom have not brass'd it so
That it is proof and bulwark against sense.

You stupid fool! Goodbye! I thought you were better. Take what you deserve. Now mother. Stop wringing your hands. Be still and sit down. Let me lay something on your heart, if it is not made of brass.

QUEEN GERTRUDE
What have I done, that thou darest wag thy tongue
In noise so rude against me?

→ seems oblivious

What have I done so terribly that you dare talk to me this way?

HAMLET
Such an act
That blurs the grace and blush of modesty,
Calls virtue hypocrite, takes off the rose
From the fair forehead of an innocent love
And sets a blister there, makes marriage-vows
As false as dicers' oaths: O, such a deed
As from the body of contraction plucks
The very soul, and sweet religion makes
A rhapsody of words: heaven's face doth glow:
Yea, this solidity and compound mass,
With tristful visage, as against the doom,
Is thought-sick at the act.

You have done such an awful act that is unforgiveable.

an unforgivable action

QUEEN GERTRUDE
Ay me, what act,
That roars so loud, and thunders in the index?

What have I done that is so awful?

HAMLET
Look here, upon this picture, and on this,
The counterfeit presentment of two brothers.
See, what a grace was seated on this brow;
Hyperion's curls; the front of Jove himself;
An eye like Mars, to threaten and command;
A station like the herald Mercury
New-lighted on a heaven-kissing hill;
A combination and a form indeed,
Where every god did seem to set his seal,
To give the world assurance of a man:
This was your husband. Look you now, what follows:
Here is your husband; like a mildew'd ear,
Blasting his wholesome brother. Have you eyes?
Could you on this fair mountain leave to feed,
And batten on this moor? Ha! have you eyes?
You cannot call it love; for at your age
The hey-day in the blood is tame, it's humble,
And waits upon the judgment: and what judgment
Would step from this to this? Sense, sure, you have,
Else could you not have motion; but sure, that sense
Is apoplex'd; for madness would not err,
Nor sense to ecstasy was ne'er so thrall'd
But it reserved some quantity of choice,
To serve in such a difference. What devil was't
That thus hath cozen'd you at hoodman-blind?
Eyes without feeling, feeling without sight,
Ears without hands or eyes, smelling sans all,
Or but a sickly part of one true sense
Could not so mope.
O shame! where is thy blush? Rebellious hell,
If thou canst mutine in a matron's bones,
To flaming youth let virtue be as wax,
And melt in her own fire: proclaim no shame
When the compulsive ardour gives the charge,
Since frost itself as actively doth burn
And reason panders will.

Imagine this...Two brothers sitting side-by-side where one is blessed by God and in the eyes of man. This man was your husband. Now the other man is horrid and capable of evil. He is your current husband. Don't you see? Why are with this man? Don't say it is love, because love fades with age and is replaced with wisdom. What persuaded you to marry this man? Don't you have any sense? You aren't even ashamed. Perhaps, I will not be ashamed either.

Explains and calls her out on the whole situation

QUEEN GERTRUDE
O Hamlet, speak no more:
Thou turn'st mine eyes into my very soul;
And there I see such black and grained spots

Oh, Hamlet, stop saying those things.
I am looking into my own wretched soul, black with sin.

So she knows?

As will not leave their tinct.

HAMLET
Nay, but to live
In the rank sweat of an enseamed bed,
Stew'd in corruption, honeying and making love
Over the nasty sty,--

Yes, and you live in a bed of sin, corrupt with love making.

[handwritten: love has corrupted her]

QUEEN GERTRUDE
O, speak to me no more;
These words, like daggers, enter in mine ears;
No more, sweet Hamlet!

Say no more. You're killing me! No more, please, Hamlet!

HAMLET
A murderer and a villain;
A slave that is not twentieth part the tithe
Of your precedent lord; a vice of kings;
A cutpurse of the empire and the rule,
That from a shelf the precious diadem stole,
And put it in his pocket!

You are married to a murderer and a villain, a shadow of your first husband, who stole the crown.

[handwritten: She married a bad person]

QUEEN GERTRUDE
No more!

No more!

HAMLET
A king of shreds and patches,--

He is a pathetic king...

Enter Ghost

[handwritten: he is being avenged]

Save me, and hover o'er me with your wings,
You heavenly guards! What would your gracious figure?

Oh, God, sending your angel to save me. What do you want?

QUEEN GERTRUDE
Alas, he's mad!

Finally, he's gone crazy!

HAMLET
Do you not come your tardy son to chide,
That, lapsed in time and passion, lets go by
The important acting of your dread command? O, say!

Please don't be upset that it has taken me so long to obey you. Tell me?

Ghost
Do not forget: this visitation
Is but to whet thy almost blunted purpose.
But, look, amazement on thy mother sits:
O, step between her and her fighting soul:
Conceit in weakest bodies strongest works:
Speak to her, Hamlet.

Don't forget your purpose. Your mother is close to breaking. Keep talking to her.

[handwritten: encourages Hamlet to keep going]

HAMLET
How is it with you, lady?

How are you doing, mother?

QUEEN GERTRUDE
Alas, how is't with you,
That you do bend your eye on vacancy
And with the incorporal air do hold discourse?
Forth at your eyes your spirits wildly peep;
And, as the sleeping soldiers in the alarm,
Your bedded hair, like life in excrements,
Starts up, and stands on end. O gentle son,
Upon the heat and flame of thy distemper

How are you? Who are you talking to? Your hair is standing on end. Calm down and tell me what are you looking at?

[handwritten: telling him to calm down]

Sprinkle cool patience. Whereon do you look?

HAMLET
On him, on him! Look you, how pale he glares!
His form and cause conjoin'd, preaching to stones,
Would make them capable. Do not look upon me;
Lest with this piteous action you convert
My stern effects: then what I have to do
Will want true colour; tears perchance for blood.

At him, at him! Look how pale he is. He could make the stones move. Don't look at me or else I will cry and be unable to kill.

QUEEN GERTRUDE
To whom do you speak this?

will be bad to kill her

Who are you talking to?

HAMLET
Do you see nothing there?

Do you not see anything?

QUEEN GERTRUDE
Nothing at all; yet all that is I see.

I don't see anything unusual.

HAMLET
Nor did you nothing hear?

And you don't hear anything?

QUEEN GERTRUDE
No, nothing but ourselves.

Nothing but us talking.

HAMLET
Why, look you there! look, how it steals away!
My father, in his habit as he lived!
Look, where he goes, even now, out at the portal!

Look over there. See how he is going away. It is my father. He looks just like he did when he was alive. Look, he's going out the door.

Exit Ghost

QUEEN GERTRUDE
This the very coinage of your brain:
This bodiless creation ecstasy
Is very cunning in.

Is it all in his head?

It is only your imagination playing tricks on you.

HAMLET
Ecstasy!
My pulse, as yours, doth temperately keep time,
And makes as healthful music: it is not madness
That I have utter'd: bring me to the test,
And I the matter will re-word; which madness
Would gambol from. Mother, for love of grace,
Lay not that mattering unction to your soul,
That not your trespass, but my madness speaks:
It will but skin and film the ulcerous place,
Whilst rank corruption, mining all within,
Infects unseen. Confess yourself to heaven;
Repent what's past; avoid what is to come;
And do not spread the compost on the weeds,
To make them ranker. Forgive me this my virtue;
For in the fatness of these pursy times
Virtue itself of vice must pardon beg,
Yea, curb and woo for leave to do him good.

*You think I am crazy!
My heart beats as well as yours. I am not mad; test me. I know exactly what I am saying. Mother, for the love of the Lord, don't blame your crimes on my madness. You will only suffer. Confess your sins to heaven and repent. Avoid the obvious outcome of your sins. Don't let this go on any longer and forgive me for trying to do good in these horrible times.*

QUEEN GERTRUDE
O Hamlet, thou hast cleft my heart in twain.

he wants her to admit her faults

Oh Hamlet, you have torn my heart in two.

HAMLET

82

O, throw away the worser part of it,
And live the purer with the other half.
Good night: but go not to mine uncle's bed;
Assume a virtue, if you have it not.
That monster, custom, who all sense doth eat,
Of habits devil, is angel yet in this,
That to the use of actions fair and good
He likewise gives a frock or livery,
That aptly is put on. Refrain to-night,
And that shall lend a kind of easiness
To the next abstinence: the next more easy;
For use almost can change the stamp of nature,
And either rein the devil, or throw him out
With wondrous potency. Once more, good night:
And when you are desirous to be bless'd,
I'll blessing beg of you. For this same lord,

Throw away the worst part of your life and live more purely. Have a good night, but do not go to my uncle's bed.

Pretend to be virtuous, if you have none. Do not give in to temptation. Start saying no to my uncle tonight. Once again, have a good night.

Pointing to POLONIUS

> I dont agree to everything he says

I do repent: but heaven hath pleased it so,
To punish me with this and this with me,
That I must be their scourge and minister.
I will bestow him, and will answer well
The death I gave him. So, again, good night.
I must be cruel, only to be kind:
Thus bad begins and worse remains behind.
One word more, good lady.

I will repent for this murder, even though it was God's will. I am only God's instrument. I know I will have to pay in the end. One other thing...

> he is responsible for the death

QUEEN GERTRUDE
What shall I do?

What would you have me do?

HAMLET
Not this, by no means, that I bid you do:
Let the bloat king tempt you again to bed;
Pinch wanton on your cheek; call you his mouse;
And let him, for a pair of reechy kisses,
Or paddling in your neck with his damn'd fingers,
Make you to ravel all this matter out,
That I essentially am not in madness,
But mad in craft. 'Twere good you let him know;
For who, that's but a queen, fair, sober, wise,
Would from a paddock, from a bat, a gib,
Such dear concernings hide? who would do so?
No, in despite of sense and secrecy,
Unpeg the basket on the house's top.
Let the birds fly, and, like the famous ape,
To try conclusions, in the basket creep,
And break your own neck down.

Whatever you do, do not let that bloated king tempt you into his bed again, call you his mouse, or pinch your cheek. Don't let him touch you with his damned fingers or convince you to think badly of me. But, what wise queen would do fall for a pig like him. Go ahead and tell him what's what, even if it means the end for you.

> confront King Claudius

QUEEN GERTRUDE
Be thou assured, if words be made of breath,
And breath of life, I have no life to breathe
What thou hast said to me.

Rest assure that I will not breathe a word of what you said tonight.

HAMLET
I must to England; you know that?

Did you know I have to go to England?

QUEEN GERTRUDE
Alack,

Oh yes, I had forgotten that, but it has been decided.

> he knows his fate

I had forgot: 'tis so concluded on.

HAMLET
There's letters seal'd: and my two schoolfellows,
Whom I will trust as I will adders fang'd,
They bear the mandate; they must sweep my way,
And marshal me to knavery. Let it work;
For 'tis the sport to have the engineer
Hoist with his own petard: and 't shall go hard
But I will delve one yard below their mines,
And blow them at the moon: O, 'tis most sweet,
When in one line two crafts directly meet.
This man shall set me packing:
I'll lug the guts into the neighbour room.
Mother, good night. Indeed this counsellor
Is now most still, most secret and most grave,
Who was in life a foolish prating knave.
Come, sir, to draw toward an end with you.
Good night, mother.

Exeunt severally, HAMLET dragging in POLONIUS

There are two sealed letters that state my two friends from school, whom I do not trust any more than a snake, will take me to England. So what? Let them try. His plan is going to blow up in his face. However, I will come out just fine. I am going to have to leave in a hurry now. I'll carry the body into the other room. Good night, Mother. This man is indeed a great counselor; he can keep secrets forever. Good night.

[handwritten: he has no trust in Rosencrentz nor Guildenstrn]

[handwritten: Interesting way to end the Act]

Act IV

Scene I

A room in the castle

Enter KING CLAUDIUS, QUEEN GERTRUDE, ROSENCRANTZ, and GUILDENSTERN

KING CLAUDIUS
There's matter in these sighs, these profound heaves:
You must translate: 'tis fit we understand them.
Where is your son?

What's wrong with you, making these deep sighs? You must tell me what's going on.
Where is Hamlet?

QUEEN GERTRUDE
Bestow this place on us a little while.

Let us have some privacy for a bit.

Exeunt ROSENCRANTZ and GUILDENSTERN

Ah, my good lord, what have I seen to-night!

You won't believe what I have seen tonight!

KING CLAUDIUS
What, Gertrude? How does Hamlet?

What Gertrude? How is Hamlet?

QUEEN GERTRUDE
Mad as the sea and wind, when both contend
Which is the mightier: in his lawless fit,
Behind the arras hearing something stir,
Whips out his rapier, cries, 'A rat, a rat!'
And, in this brainish apprehension, kills
The unseen good old man.

He is completely crazy. He heard something behind the curtains and in a rage he drew his sword and cried, "A rat, a rat!" Then he killed the old man.

KING CLAUDIUS
O heavy deed!
It had been so with us, had we been there:
His liberty is full of threats to all;
To you yourself, to us, to every one.
Alas, how shall this bloody deed be answer'd?
It will be laid to us, whose providence
Should have kept short, restrain'd and out of haunt,
This mad young man: but so much was our love,
We would not understand what was most fit;
But, like the owner of a foul disease,
To keep it from divulging, let it feed
Even on the pith of Life. Where is he gone?

Oh, what a terrible thing!
It would have been me, if I had been there. His freedom is a threat to everyone. How are we going to answer this murder? It is our responsibility to restrain this young madman. We loved him so much we could not see clearly. Now, this has happened like a contagious disease. Where is he, now?

QUEEN GERTRUDE
To draw apart the body he hath kill'd:
O'er whom his very madness, like some ore
Among a mineral of metals base,
Shows itself pure; he weeps for what is done.

He has gone to dispose of the body. He is sorry for what he has done.

KING CLAUDIUS
O Gertrude, come away!
The sun no sooner shall the mountains touch,
But we will ship him hence: and this vile deed
We must, with all our majesty and skill,
Both countenance and excuse. Ho, Guildenstern!

Oh Gertrude, be sensible.
We must send him away as soon as the sun rises. We will have to find some way to excuse this murder. Hey, Guildenstern.

Re-enter ROSENCRANTZ and GUILDENSTERN

[handwritten annotations: What is going on? / Says he is utterly insane / Says their love for him blinded them / Still will send him away]

Friends both, go join you with some further aid:
Hamlet in madness hath Polonius slain,
And from his mother's closet hath he dragg'd him.
Go seek him out; speak fair, and bring the body
Into the chapel. I pray you, haste in this.

Exeunt ROSENCRANTZ and GUILDENSTERN

Come, Gertrude, we'll call up our wisest friends;
And let them know, both what we mean to do,
And what's untimely done. O, come away!
My soul is full of discord and dismay.

Exeunt

*Gentlemen, both of you go find some people to help Hamlet.
Out of his madness, he has killed Polonius.
Now he is dragging the body out of his mother's bedroom.
Go speak to him and bring the body to the church. Hurry,
please.*

*Come on, Gertrude, we'll get our wisest friends to let them know
what we are doing and what has been done. Let's go! My soul is
heavy.*

the word will go around about the murder of Polonius

Scene II

Another room in the castle

Enter HAMLET

HAMLET
Safely stowed.

There, the body is safely stowed away.

the body is disposed of

ROSENCRANTZ: GUILDENSTERN:
[Within]
Hamlet! Lord Hamlet!

Hamlet! Lord Hamlet!

HAMLET
What noise? who calls on Hamlet?
O, here they come.

What is that noise? Who is calling me? Here they come.

Enter ROSENCRANTZ and GUILDENSTERN

ROSENCRANTZ
What have you done, my lord, with the dead body?

What have you done with the body, my lord?

HAMLET
Compounded it with dust, whereto 'tis kin.

Put it in the dirt.

ROSENCRANTZ
Tell us where 'tis, that we may take it thence
And bear it to the chapel.

Tell us where it is so we can take it to the church.

HAMLET
Do not believe it.

I don't believe it.

a very religious duo

ROSENCRANTZ
Believe what?

Believe what?

HAMLET
That I can keep your counsel and not mine own.
Besides, to be demanded of a sponge! what
replication should be made by the son of a king?

That I can trust you and expose my secret. Besides, who are you, a mere sponge, to command the son of a king?

ROSENCRANTZ
Take you me for a sponge, my lord?

You think I am a sponge, my lord?

calling their purpose out

HAMLET
Ay, sir, that soaks up the king's countenance, his
rewards, his authorities. But such officers do the
king best service in the end: he keeps them, like
an ape, in the corner of his jaw; first mouthed, to
be last swallowed: when he needs what you have
gleaned, it is but squeezing you, and, sponge, you
shall be dry again.

Yes sir, that soaks up whatever the king says and does. He is just using you and when he is done, you will be left high and dry.

ROSENCRANTZ
I understand you not, my lord.

I don't understand, my lord.

HAMLET
I am glad of it: a knavish speech sleeps in a foolish ear.

I am glad. You are too foolish to understand.

↳ calls them stupid

ROSENCRANTZ
My lord, you must tell us where the body is, and go
with us to the king.

HAMLET
The body is with the king, but the king is not with
the body. The king is a thing--

GUILDENSTERN
A thing, my lord!

HAMLET
Of nothing: bring me to him. Hide fox, and all after.

Exeunt

My lord, you must tell us where the body is and go with us to the king.

The body is with the king, but he is not there. The king is just a thing...

A thing, my lord!

He is a thing of no importance. Take me to him and tell him to hide.

he intends on
continuing his
plan of revenge

Scene III

Another room in the castle

Enter KING CLAUDIUS, attended

KING CLAUDIUS
I have sent to seek him, and to find the body.
How dangerous is it that this man goes loose!
Yet must not we put the strong law on him:
He's loved of the distracted multitude,
Who like not in their judgment, but their eyes;
And where tis so, the offender's scourge is weigh'd,
But never the offence. To bear all smooth and even,
This sudden sending him away must seem
Deliberate pause: diseases desperate grown
By desperate appliance are relieved,
Or not at all.

I have sent someone to find him and bring back the body. He is dangerous on the loose. But, we can't put the law on him too strongly. He's very loved by the people, and they will not take too kindly to his punishment. The only way to handle this is to send him away. Desperate times call for desperate measures.

Confirmed of the dangers that Hamlet poses

Enter ROSENCRANTZ

How now! what hath befall'n?

What's going on?

ROSENCRANTZ
Where the dead body is bestow'd, my lord,
We cannot get from him.

He won't tell us where the body is hidden.

KING CLAUDIUS
But where is he?

they failed their task

Where is he?

ROSENCRANTZ
Without, my lord; guarded, to know your pleasure.

He is being guarded outside.

KING CLAUDIUS
Bring him before us.

Bring him here.

ROSENCRANTZ
Ho, Guildenstern! bring in my lord.

Hey, Guildenstern! Bring in my lord.

Enter HAMLET and GUILDENSTERN

KING CLAUDIUS
Now, Hamlet, where's Polonius?

Now, Hamlet, where's Polonius?

HAMLET
At supper.

he is lying

He is at supper.

KING CLAUDIUS
At supper! where?

Where at supper?

HAMLET
Not where he eats, but where he is eaten: a certain
convocation of politic worms are e'en at him. Your
worm is your only emperor for diet: we fat all
creatures else to fat us, and we fat ourselves for
maggots: your fat king and your lean beggar is but
variable service, two dishes, but to one table:
that's the end.

He is not eating, but being eaten by worms. We all become worm food in the end.

nevermind, says the worms eat him

KING CLAUDIUS
Alas, alas!

HAMLET
A man may fish with the worm that hath eat of a
king, and eat of the fish that hath fed of that worm.

KING CLAUDIUS
What dost you mean by this?

HAMLET
Nothing but to show you how a king may go a
progress through the guts of a beggar.

KING CLAUDIUS
Where is Polonius?

HAMLET
In heaven; send hither to see: if your messenger
find him not there, seek him i' the other place
yourself. But indeed, if you find him not within
this month, you shall nose him as you go up the
stairs into the lobby.

KING CLAUDIUS
Go seek him there.

To some Attendants

HAMLET
He will stay till ye come.

Exeunt Attendants

KING CLAUDIUS
Hamlet, this deed, for thine especial safety,--
Which we do tender, as we dearly grieve
For that which thou hast done,--must send thee hence
With fiery quickness: therefore prepare thyself;
The bark is ready, and the wind at help,
The associates tend, and every thing is bent
For England.

HAMLET
For England!

KING CLAUDIUS
Ay, Hamlet.

HAMLET
Good.

KING CLAUDIUS
So is it, if thou knew'st our purposes.

HAMLET
I see a cherub that sees them. But, come; for England!
Farewell, dear mother.

KING CLAUDIUS
Thy loving father, Hamlet.

Enough, enough!

*The same worm that eats a king may become food for a fish
which serves as the dinner for a cat.*

What are you talking about?

*I just want to show you what happens to a king's body after he is
gone.*

Where is Polonius?

*In heaven. Send someone to see and if your messenger does not
find him there, go look for yourself in the other place. If you
can't find him there, you'll be able to smell him in the next
month as you go into the lobby.*

Go look there.

He's not going anywhere.

*For this deed you have committed, you are going to have to
leave for awhile. You must be ready quickly, so go prepare
yourself. The boat is ready to take you and your associates to
England.*

For England!

Yes, Hamlet.

Good.

You act as if you knew what we were going to do.

*A little angel told me. So, off to England.
Farewell, dear mother.*

I am your loving father, Hamlet.

[handwritten annotations:]
a very interesting extended metaphor

that was very much to the point

saying Hamlet is to be sent away

Is very okay with leaving

HAMLET

My mother: father and mother is man and wife;
man and wife is one flesh; and so, my mother.
Come, for England!

Exit

KING CLAUDIUS

Follow him at foot; tempt him with speed aboard;
Delay it not; I'll have him hence to-night:
Away! for every thing is seal'd and done
That else leans on the affair: pray you, make haste.

Exeunt ROSENCRANTZ and GUILDENSTERN

And, England, if my love thou hold'st at aught--
As my great power thereof may give thee sense,
Since yet thy cicatrice looks raw and red
After the Danish sword, and thy free awe
Pays homage to us--thou mayst not coldly set
Our sovereign process; which imports at full,
By letters congruing to that effect,
The present death of Hamlet. Do it, England;
For like the hectic in my blood he rages,
And thou must cure me: till I know 'tis done,
Howe'er my haps, my joys were ne'er begun.

Exit

*You're my mother. Like it says, when a man takes a wife,
they become of one flesh. So, you are my mother.
Come on, off to England!*

*Follow him closely, and see he gets on board quickly. Don't
delay. I want him gone tonight.*

*And, while in England, if you love me, and you should
considering what all the Danes have done in the past,
you will not hesitate to kill Hamlet. Obey me, England, and cure
me of my sickness. I will not be well until it is done.*

[handwritten: wants to rid of him as quickly as possible]

[handwritten: killing Hamlet can only help him]

92

Scene IV

A plain in Denmark

Enter FORTINBRAS, a Captain, and Soldiers, marching

PRINCE FORTINBRAS
Go, captain, from me greet the Danish king;
Tell him that, by his licence, Fortinbras
Craves the conveyance of a promised march
Over his kingdom. You know the rendezvous.
If that his majesty would aught with us,
We shall express our duty in his eye;
And let him know so.

> *Go, Captain, and greet the Danish king. Tell him that I would like to march through his kingdom, with his permission. You know the place. Let him know we will grant him his favor.*

[handwritten: In this the trouble of the regions?]

Captain
I will do't, my lord.

> *I will do it, my lord.*

PRINCE FORTINBRAS
Go softly on.

> *Go quietly.*

Exeunt FORTINBRAS and Soldiers

Enter HAMLET, ROSENCRANTZ, GUILDENSTERN, and others

HAMLET
Good sir, whose powers are these?

> *Hello sir. Whose army is this?*

Captain
They are of Norway, sir.

> *They are from Norway, sir.*

HAMLET
How purposed, sir, I pray you?

> *What is their purpose, sir?*

Captain
Against some part of Poland.

> *They are on their way to Poland.*

HAMLET
Who commands them, sir?

> *Who is in command, sir?*

[handwritten: Norway is attacking Poland]

Captain
The nephews to old Norway, Fortinbras.

> *The nephew to the old king of Norway, Fortinbras.*

HAMLET
Goes it against the main of Poland, sir,
Or for some frontier?

> *Is he attacking the heart of Poland or some part of it?*

Captain
Truly to speak, and with no addition,
We go to gain a little patch of ground
That hath in it no profit but the name.
To pay five ducats, five, I would not farm it;
Nor will it yield to Norway or the Pole
A ranker rate, should it be sold in fee.

> *We are going to gain a little land that I wouldn't pay five dollars to farm.*

[handwritten: a very poor part of the country]

HAMLET
Why, then the Polack never will defend it.

> *Well, then the Poles will never defend it*

Captain
Yes, it is already garrison'd.

Yes they will. It is already guarded.

HAMLET
Two thousand souls and twenty thousand ducats
Will not debate the question of this straw:
This is the imposthume of much wealth and peace,
That inward breaks, and shows no cause without
Why the man dies. I humbly thank you, sir.

Two thousand souls and twenty thousand dollars will not settle this dispute. This is the result of too much money and peace. It is quite pointless. Thank you for the information, sir.

[handwritten: money and peace caused this dispute]

Captain
God be wi' you, sir.

God be with you, sir.

Exit

ROSENCRANTZ
Wilt please you go, my lord?

Are you ready to go, my lord?

HAMLET
I'll be with you straight go a little before.

Go ahead. I'll be there soon.

Exeunt all except HAMLET

How all occasions do inform against me,
And spur my dull revenge! What is a man,
If his chief good and market of his time
Be but to sleep and feed? a beast, no more.
Sure, he that made us with such large discourse,
Looking before and after, gave us not
That capability and god-like reason
To fust in us unused. Now, whether it be
Bestial oblivion, or some craven scruple
Of thinking too precisely on the event,
A thought which, quarter'd, hath but one part wisdom
And ever three parts coward, I do not know
Why yet I live to say 'This thing's to do;'
Sith I have cause and will and strength and means
To do't. Examples gross as earth exhort me:
Witness this army of such mass and charge
Led by a delicate and tender prince,
Whose spirit with divine ambition puff'd
Makes mouths at the invisible event,
Exposing what is mortal and unsure
To all that fortune, death and danger dare,
Even for an egg-shell. Rightly to be great
Is not to stir without great argument,
But greatly to find quarrel in a straw
When honour's at the stake. How stand I then,
That have a father kill'd, a mother stain'd,
Excitements of my reason and my blood,
And let all sleep? while, to my shame, I see
The imminent death of twenty thousand men,
That, for a fantasy and trick of fame,
Go to their graves like beds, fight for a plot
Whereon the numbers cannot try the cause,
Which is not tomb enough and continent
To hide the slain? O, from this time forth,
My thoughts be bloody, or be nothing worth!

Everything is telling me to hurry up and get on with my plan. What is a man if he only eats and sleeps? He is no more than a beast. God did not create us to waste our minds and abilities. There is a reason for my existence. Let me not ignore this opportunity, a silly young prince led by selfish ambition is offering his life for the sake of honor. I will not have another idle thought. I will think of nothing but revenge.

[handwritten: when will he complete his vengence?]

[handwritten: revenge is the only thing on his mind]

Exit

Scene V

Elsinore. A room in the castle

Enter QUEEN GERTRUDE, HORATIO, and a Gentleman

QUEEN GERTRUDE
I will not speak with her.

[handwritten: weird to include a random Gentleman]

I will not speak with her.

Gentleman
She is importunate, indeed distract:
Her mood will needs be pitied.

She won't go away. She needs to be pitied.

QUEEN GERTRUDE
What would she have?

What does she want?

Gentleman
She speaks much of her father; says she hears
There's tricks i' the world; and hems, and beats her heart;
Spurns enviously at straws; speaks things in doubt,
That carry but half sense: her speech is nothing,
Yet the unshaped use of it doth move
The hearers to collection; they aim at it,
And botch the words up fit to their own thoughts;
Which, as her winks, and nods, and gestures
yield them,
Indeed would make one think there might be thought,
Though nothing sure, yet much unhappily.

[handwritten: I believe that this refers to Ophelia]

She talks about her father. She says there are tricks in the world and cries and beats her heart. She is talking out of her head. People listen to her and hear what they want. It seems she is trying to tell something horrible.

HORATIO
'Twere good she were spoken with; for she may strew
Dangerous conjectures in ill-breeding minds.

She needs to be spoken with because she is causing people to think the unthinkable.

QUEEN GERTRUDE
Let her come in.

[handwritten: Is she encouraging poorly?]

Bring her in.

Exit HORATIO

To my sick soul, as sin's true nature is,
Each toy seems prologue to some great amiss:
So full of artless jealousy is guilt,
It spills itself in fearing to be spilt.

Everything within me tells me something awful about to happen. Perhaps it is just my guilt eating away at me.

Re-enter HORATIO, with OPHELIA

OPHELIA
Where is the beauteous majesty of Denmark?

Where is her majesty of Denmark?

QUEEN GERTRUDE
How now, Ophelia!

How are you, Ophelia?

OPHELIA
[Sings]
How should I your true love know
From another one?
By his cockle hat and staff,
And his sandal shoon.

[handwritten: she feels something bad coming]

*How can you tell your true love from another?
By his hat and walking stick or his shoe?*

QUEEN GERTRUDE
Alas, sweet lady, what imports this song?

What brings about this song?

OPHELIA
Say you? nay, pray you, mark.

Did you say something? No? Just listen.

Sings

He is dead and gone, lady,
He is dead and gone;
He is dead and gone;
At his head a grass-green turf,
At his heels a stone.

He is dead and gone, lady.
Dead and gone. Grass grows over his head and a stone is placed
at his foot.

A very melancholy song

QUEEN GERTRUDE
Nay, but, Ophelia,--

Stop, Ophelia...

OPHELIA
Pray you, mark.

I beg you to listen.

Sings

White his shroud as the mountain snow,--

His shroud is as white as the mountain snow...

Enter KING CLAUDIUS

QUEEN GERTRUDE
Alas, look here, my lord.

At last, look at this girl, my lord.

they think she needs help

OPHELIA
[Sings]
Larded with sweet flowers
Which bewept to the grave did go
With true-love showers.

Covered in sweet flowers which were tossed to the ground by
true love showers.

KING CLAUDIUS
How do you, pretty lady?

How are you, pretty lady?

OPHELIA
Well, God 'ild you! They say the owl was a baker's
daughter. Lord, we know what we are, but know not
what we may be. God be at your table!

I'm well, and may God give you yours. They say the baker's
daughter was an owl. My lord, we know what we are, but not
what we are to become. May God be at your table.

KING CLAUDIUS
Conceit upon her father.

She is thinking about her father.

A very profound line

OPHELIA
Pray you, let's have no words of this; but when they
ask you what it means, say you this:

I beg you to not talk about that. But, when asked tell them the
song means:

Sings

To-morrow is Saint Valentine's day,
All in the morning betime,
And I a maid at your window,
To be your Valentine.
Then up he rose, and donn'd his clothes,
And dupp'd the chamber-door;
Let in the maid, that out a maid
Never departed more.

Tomorrow is Saint Valentine's day,
and in the early morning, I will be at your window to be your
Valentine. Then he got up and dressed and opened the bedroom
door. He let in a maid, but let out a woman.

that should be a time of joy and love

KING CLAUDIUS
Pretty Ophelia!

OPHELIA
Indeed, la, without an oath, I'll make an end on't:

Sings

By Gis and by Saint Charity,
Alack, and fie for shame!
Young men will do't, if they come to't;
By cock, they are to blame.
Quoth she, before you tumbled me,
You promised me to wed.
So would I ha' done, by yonder sun,
An thou hadst not come to my bed.

KING CLAUDIUS
How long hath she been thus?

OPHELIA
I hope all will be well. We must be patient:
but I I hope all will be well. We must be patient:
but I cannot choose but weep, to think they should lay him
i' the cold ground. My brother shall know of it:
and so I thank you for your good counsel. Come, my
coach! Good night, ladies; good night, sweet ladies;
good night, good night.

Exit

KING CLAUDIUS
Follow her close; give her good watch,

I pray you.

Exit HORATIO

O, this is the poison of deep grief; it springs
All from her father's death. O Gertrude, Gertrude,
When sorrows come, they come not single spies
But in battalions. First, her father slain:
Next, your son gone; and he most violent author
Of his own just remove: the people muddied,
Thick and unwholesome in their thoughts and whispers,
For good Polonius' death; and we have done but greenly,
In hugger-mugger to inter him: poor Ophelia
Divided from herself and her fair judgment,
Without the which we are pictures, or mere beasts:
Last, and as much containing as all these,
Her brother is in secret come from France;
Feeds on his wonder, keeps himself in clouds,
And wants not buzzers to infect his ear
With pestilent speeches of his father's death;
Wherein necessity, of matter beggar'd,
Will nothing stick our person to arraign
In ear and ear. O my dear Gertrude, this,
Like to a murdering-piece, in many places
Gives me superfluous death.

A noise within

Pretty Ophelia!

I promise, I will end it soon...

By Jesus and Saint Charity, shame young men who must do it. They are to blame. She said you promised to marry me before you brought me into your bed, but now you won't because I came to your bed.

How long has she been like this?

I hope everything works out well. We must wait and see. But I can't help crying, thinking about his body in the cold ground. My brother will be told about this, so thank you. Thank you for your advice. Come on, Driver. Good night, sweet ladies. Good night.

Follow her closely and watch her.

This is the result of deep grief. It comes from the death of her father. Sadness comes in swells. First, her father is killed. Next, your son is sent away by his own doings. Poor Ophelia did not get to mourn her father properly; we buried him so quickly. Now, the people are spreading nasty rumors about his death. She is now crazy with grief, and her brother who has secretly returned from France hears the gossip. He is going to think I killed his father, which is killing me.

[handwritten annotations: assures him She is almost done; She is clearly experiencing grief; grief takes a great toll on people; She is no longer herself]

97

QUEEN GERTRUDE
Alack, what noise is this?
KING CLAUDIUS
Where are my Switzers? Let them guard the door.

Enter another Gentleman

What is the matter?

Gentleman
Save yourself, my lord:
The ocean, overpeering of his list,
Eats not the flats with more impetuous haste
Than young Laertes, in a riotous head,
O'erbears your officers. The rabble call him lord;
And, as the world were now but to begin,
Antiquity forgot, custom not known,
The ratifiers and props of every word,
They cry 'Choose we: Laertes shall be king:'
Caps, hands, and tongues, applaud it to the clouds:
'Laertes shall be king, Laertes king!'

QUEEN GERTRUDE
How cheerfully on the false trail they cry!
O, this is counter, you false Danish dogs!

KING CLAUDIUS
The doors are broke.

Noise within

Enter LAERTES, armed; Danes following

LAERTES
Where is this king? Sirs, stand you all without.

Danes
No, let's come in.

LAERTES
I pray you, give me leave.

Danes
We will, we will.

They retire without the door

LAERTES
I thank you: keep the door. O thou vile king,
Give me my father!

QUEEN GERTRUDE
Calmly, good Laertes.

LAERTES
That drop of blood that's calm proclaims me bastard,
Cries cuckold to my father, brands the harlot
Even here, between the chaste unsmirched brow
Of my true mother.

What was that?

Where are my guards? Let them stand by the door.

What is going on?

Save yourself, my lord.
Young Laertes is leading a riotous group across the lowlands. The crowds call him lord and shout, "We want Laertes to be our king," like they have forgotten our customs. They are throwing their caps in the air and cheering, "King Laertes."

They sound so cheerful, but they are after the wrong dog!

The doors are breaking.

Where is the king? Sirs, surround the area.

No, let's go in.

I ask that you give me a moment.

We will.

Thank you. Guard the door. Oh you vile king, give me my father!

Calm down, good Laertes.

I have one drop of blood that's calm and it calls me a bastard-child, my father a fool, and my mother a harlot.

[handwritten annotations] wants the guards to be prepared

[handwritten] want to overthrow Claudius

[handwritten] he seemed so insignificant

[handwritten] he knows

[handwritten] he wants his dead dad

KING CLAUDIUS
What is the cause, Laertes,
That thy rebellion looks so giant-like?
Let him go, Gertrude; do not fear our person:
There's such divinity doth hedge a king,
That treason can but peep to what it would,
Acts little of his will. Tell me, Laertes,
Why thou art thus incensed. Let him go, Gertrude.
Speak, man.

What is wrong, Laertes?
Why are you leading this giant rebellion?
Let him go, Gertrude. We have no need to fear, because God
will protect us against traitors. Tell me, Laertes, why are you so
angry? Let him go, Gertrude. Speak, man.

[handwritten: thinks God will protec them]

LAERTES
Where is my father?

Where is my father?

KING CLAUDIUS
Dead.

He is dead.

QUEEN GERTRUDE
But not by him.

But the king didn't kill him.

[handwritten: Gertrude reassures Laertes]

KING CLAUDIUS
Let him demand his fill.

Let him make his demands.

LAERTES
How came he dead? I'll not be juggled with:
To hell, allegiance! vows, to the blackest devil!
Conscience and grace, to the profoundest pit!
I dare damnation. To this point I stand,
That both the worlds I give to negligence,
Let come what comes; only I'll be revenged
Most thoroughly for my father.

How did he die? I will not be lied to or threatened with hell. I
don't care what happens anymore. I just want revenge for my
father.

KING CLAUDIUS
Who shall stay you?

[handwritten: revenge is a common theme]

Who's controlling you?

LAERTES
My will, not all the world:
And for my means, I'll husband them so well,
They shall go far with little.

I am acting by my will alone, and I will use whatever means I
have against you.

KING CLAUDIUS
Good Laertes,
If you desire to know the certainty
If you desire to know the certainty
Of your dear father's death, is't writ in your revenge,
That, swoopstake, you will draw both friend and foe,
Winner and loser?

Good Laertes,
if you want to know the details of your father's death despite
hurting his enemies and his friends?

LAERTES
None but his enemies.

[handwritten: Warning him of the risks]

No, only his enemies.

KING CLAUDIUS
Will you know them then?

Do you know his enemies?

LAERTES
To his good friends thus wide I'll ope my arms;
And like the kind life-rendering pelican,
Repast them with my blood.

I will open my arms to his friends like a mother bird. I will die
for them.

KING CLAUDIUS
Why, now you speak
Like a good child and a true gentleman.

Now, you're talking like a good child and gentleman. I am
innocent of your father's death, and quite frankly I am

That I am guiltless of your father's death,
And am most sensible in grief for it,
It shall as level to your judgment pierce
As day does to your eye.

still grieving.

Danes
[Within]
Let her come in.

[handwritten] proclaims his innocence

Let her in.

LAERTES
How now! what noise is that?

What's going on?

Re-enter OPHELIA

O heat, dry up my brains! tears seven times salt,
Burn out the sense and virtue of mine eye!
By heaven, thy madness shall be paid by weight,
Till our scale turn the beam. O rose of May!
Dear maid, kind sister, sweet Ophelia!
O heavens! is't possible, a young maid's wits
Should be as moral as an old man's life?
Nature is fine in love, and where 'tis fine,
It sends some precious instance of itself
After the thing it loves.

Oh heat, dry up my brains and salty tears sting my eyes. I swear I will get revenge for my sweet sister's madness. Oh sweet rose! Dear sweet sister, Ophelia! My sister has lost her mind over our father's death.

[handwritten] Is upset that his sister lost her mind

OPHELIA
[Sings]
They bore him barefaced on the bier;
Hey non nonny, nonny, hey nonny;
And in his grave rain'd many a tear:--
Fare you well, my dove!

They carried him away in his coffin. Hey non nonny, hey nonny. And on his grave, cried many a tear. Good bye, my dove!

LAERTES
Hadst thou thy wits, and didst persuade revenge,
It could not move thus.

If you had your sanity and persuaded me to take revenge, I would not be as moved as I am now.

OPHELIA
[Sings]
You must sing a-down a-down,
An you call him a-down-a.
O, how the wheel becomes it! It is the false
steward, that stole his master's daughter.

[handwritten] Interesting

You must sing a-down, a-down. And you call him a-down-a. Oh, how the wheels turn around, that stole his master's daughter.

LAERTES
This nothing's more than matter.

[handwritten] that she sings of all of this

This means more than sensible talk.

OPHELIA
There's rosemary, that's for remembrance; pray,
love, remember: and there is pansies. that's for thoughts.

Rosemary is for remembrance. Remember. There are pansies for thoughts.

LAERTES
A document in madness, thoughts and remembrance fitted.

She is simply mad with memories.

OPHELIA
There's fennel for you, and columbines: there's rue
for you; and here's some for me: we may call it
herb-grace o' Sundays: O you must wear your rue with
a difference. There's a daisy: I would give you
some violets, but they withered all when my father
died: they say he made a good end,--

Here are fennel and columbines for you. And here is rue for you and me. There is a daisy and violets, but they withered up when my father died. He died well.

[handwritten] compares death of flowers to father

Sings

For bonny sweet Robin is all my joy.
LAERTES
Thought and affliction, passion, hell itself,
She turns to favour and to prettiness.

OPHELIA
[Sings]
And will he not come again?
And will he not come again?
No, no, he is dead:
Go to thy death-bed:
He never will come again.
His beard was as white as snow,
All flaxen was his poll:
He is gone, he is gone,
And we cast away moan:
God ha' mercy on his soul!
And of all Christian souls, I pray God. God be wi' ye.

Exit

LAERTES
Do you see this, O God?

KING CLAUDIUS
Laertes, I must commune with your grief,
Or you deny me right. Go but apart,
Make choice of whom your wisest friends you will.
And they shall hear and judge 'twixt you and me:
If by direct or by collateral hand
They find us touch'd, we will our kingdom give,
Our crown, our life, and all that we can ours,
To you in satisfaction, but if not,
Be you content to lend your patience to us,
And we shall jointly labour with your soul
To give it due content.

LAERTES
Let this be so;
His means of death, his obscure funeral--
No trophy, sword, nor hatchment o'er his bones,
No noble rite nor formal ostentation--
Cry to be heard, as 'twere from heaven to earth,
That I must call't in question.

KING CLAUDIUS
So you shall;
And where the offence is let the great axe fall.
I pray you, go with me.

Exeunt

The sweet robin is my joy.

Despite her affliction, she is focusing on what is pretty.

And will he come again? Will he come again? No, no he is dead, and in his death-bed. He will never come again. His beard is white as snow, and his hair was white, too. He is gone, gone, and we moan, "God have mercy on his soul!" And all the Christian souls, I pray God be with you.

Do you see this, God?

Laertes, don't deny me my grief. Go and find your wisest friends to listen to both of us and judge between you and me. If they find me at fault for your father's death, then I will give you the kingdom. If they find me innocent, then I will work to satisfy your need to know about your father's death. But, you must be patient.

Fine, but I need to know how he died and why there wasn't a proper funeral. Why was it kept so quiet?

And, so you shall. May justice prevail. Go with me, now.

[handwritten notes: the significance of beauty; very religious aspect; Claudius is very confident; thinks the death will be justified]

Scene VI

Another room in the castle

Enter HORATIO and a Servant

HORATIO
What are they that would speak with me?

Who are the people who want to speak with me?

Servant
Sailors, sir: they say they have letters for you.

Sailors, sir. They have letters for you.

HORATIO
Let them come in.

Let them come in.

Exit Servant

I do not know from what part of the world
I should be greeted, if not from Lord Hamlet.

I do not know who else would be sending me a letter from abroad, except Hamlet.

Enter Sailors

First Sailor
God bless you, sir.

God bless you, sir.

HORATIO
Let him bless thee too.

May he bless you, too.

First Sailor
He shall, sir, an't please him. There's a letter for
you, sir; it comes from the ambassador that was
bound for England; if your name be Horatio, as I am
let to know it is.

*He will, sir, if it pleases him. Here is a letter for you, sir.
It comes from the ambassador, Lord Hamlet. If you are Horatio,
let me know.*

he only knows Hamlet who is abroad

It is Hamlet

HORATIO
[Reads]
'Horatio, when thou shalt have overlooked
this, give these fellows some means to the king:
they have letters for him. Ere we were two days old
at sea, a pirate of very warlike appointment gave us
chase. Finding ourselves too slow of sail, we put on
a compelled valour, and in the grapple I boarded
them: on the instant they got clear of our ship; so
I alone became their prisoner. They have dealt with
me like thieves of mercy: but they knew what they
did; I am to do a good turn for them. Let the king
have the letters I have sent; and repair thou to me
with as much speed as thou wouldst fly death. I
have words to speak in thine ear will make thee
dumb; yet are they much too light for the bore of
the matter. These good fellows will bring thee
where I am. Rosencrantz and Guildenstern hold their
course for England: of them I have much to tell
thee. Farewell.
'He that thou knowest thine, HAMLET.'
Come, I will make you way for these your letters;
And do't the speedier, that you may direct me
To him from whom you brought them.

*"Dear Horatio, when you have looked at this letter send the
message to the king. We were at sea only two days when a pirate
ship overtook us. We tried to escape, but were too slow, so we
fought. I am now the lone prisoner on board. They have treated
me well, and want me to do them a favor. Please come to me as
quickly as you can. I have much to tell you. These messengers
will bring you to me. Rosencrantz and Guildenstern are still on
their way to England. I have much to tell you about them. Yours
truly, Hamlet." Come men. I'll show you where to take these
letters, so you can take me to Hamlet.*

Hamlet seems to be in trouble, Horatio to help him

Exeunt

Scene VII

Another room in the castle

Enter KING CLAUDIUS and LAERTES

KING CLAUDIUS
Now must your conscience my acquaintance seal,
And you must put me in your heart for friend,
Sith you have heard, and with a knowing ear,
That he which hath your noble father slain
Pursued my life.

Now you must believe that I am your friend, since the man who killed your father was trying to kill me.

LAERTES
It well appears: but tell me
Why you proceeded not against these feats,
So crimeful and so capital in nature,
As by your safety, wisdom, all things else,
You mainly were stirr'd up.

It appears so, but tell me why didn't you do anything about it.

[handwritten: Claudius very much seems like the innocent type]

KING CLAUDIUS
O, for two special reasons;
Which may to you, perhaps, seem much unsinew'd,
But yet to me they are strong. The queen his mother
Lives almost by his looks; and for myself--
My virtue or my plague, be it either which--
She's so conjunctive to my life and soul,
That, as the star moves not but in his sphere,
I could not but by her. The other motive,
Why to a public count I might not go,
Is the great love the general gender bear him;
Who, dipping all his faults in their affection,
Would, like the spring that turneth wood to stone,
Convert his gyves to graces; so that my arrows,
Too slightly timber'd for so loud a wind,
Would have reverted to my bow again,
And not where I had aim'd them.

I have two reasons, but you may think they are weak. First the queen is his mother, and she is devoted to him. She is a great part of my life, and I don't think I could live without her. The other reason is the people of Denmark love him. I could not do anything to him without them revolting.

[handwritten: proclaims his love for the queen]

LAERTES
And so have I a noble father lost;
A sister driven into desperate terms,
Whose worth, if praises may go back again,
Stood challenger on mount of all the age
For her perfections: but my revenge will come.

So, I have lost a noble father, and my sister has been driven insane. I will get my revenge in the end.

KING CLAUDIUS
Break not your sleeps for that: you must not think
That we are made of stuff so flat and dull
That we can let our beard be shook with danger
And think it pastime. You shortly shall hear more:
I loved your father, and we love ourself;
And that, I hope, will teach you to imagine—

Don't worry about that. You mustn't think that I am so old and dull that I can sit idly by while being threatened. You will soon hear more about my plans. I loved your father and I love myself enough to...

[handwritten: Is losing all members of his family]

Enter a Messenger

How now! what news?

What's going on? Do you have news for me?

Messenger

104

Letters, my lord, from Hamlet:
This to your majesty; this to the queen.

Letters, my lord, from Hamlet. This is for the queen.

KING CLAUDIUS
From Hamlet! who brought them?

Very concerning for him

Letters from Hamlet? Who brought them?

Messenger
Sailors, my lord, they say; I saw them not:
They were given me by Claudio; he received them
Of him that brought them.

Sailors, my lord, although I didn't see them. The letters were brought by Claudio.

KING CLAUDIUS
Laertes, you shall hear them. Leave us.

Laertes, you can listen. Leave us.

Exit Messenger

Reads

'High and mighty, You shall know I am set naked on
your kingdom. To-morrow shall I beg leave to see
your kingly eyes: when I shall, first asking your
pardon thereunto, recount the occasion of my sudden
and more strange return. 'HAMLET.'
What should this mean? Are all the rest come back?
Or is it some abuse, and no such thing?

"High and mighty, You will know that I am returning to Denmark and I ask that you will see me. I apologize for my actions. I will tell you how I came back to Denmark so suddenly. Hamlet." What does this mean? Is everyone back or is this some joke?

LAERTES
Know you the hand?

the letter sent from Hamlet

Do you recognize the handwriting?

KING CLAUDIUS
'Tis Hamlets character. 'Naked!
And in a postscript here, he says 'alone.'
Can you advise me?

It's Hamlet's. Here he states he wants to see me alone. What do you think?

LAERTES
I'm lost in it, my lord. But let him come;
It warms the very sickness in my heart,
That I shall live and tell him to his teeth,
'Thus didest thou.'

I don't understand it, my lord. But let him come. It warms my heart and sets my soul ablaze to know that I will live to tell him to his face what he has done.

KING CLAUDIUS
If it be so, Laertes--
As how should it be so? how otherwise?--
Will you be ruled by me?

wants Hamlet to feel guilty

If it is to be, Laertes, will you let me guide you? Of course you will.

LAERTES
Ay, my lord;
So you will not o'errule me to a peace.

Yes, my lord.
Just don't think I will be persuaded to act peacefully.

KING CLAUDIUS
To thine own peace. If he be now return'd,
As checking at his voyage, and that he means
No more to undertake it, I will work him
To an exploit, now ripe in my device,
Under the which he shall not choose but fall:
And for his death no wind of blame shall breathe,
But even his mother shall uncharge the practise
And call it accident.

No, just to give you some inner peace. If he is back without any means to continue on his trip, then I am going to put in place a plan that will surely kill him. Even his mother will think it was an accident.

LAERTES
My lord, I will be ruled;

Intend on killing Hamlet

My lord, I will follow your lead,

The rather, if you could devise it so
That I might be the organ.

but I would like to be the instrument of Hamlet's death, if possible.

KING CLAUDIUS
It falls right.
You have been talk'd of since your travel much,
And that in Hamlet's hearing, for a quality
Wherein, they say, you shine: your sum of parts
Did not together pluck such envy from him
As did that one, and that, in my regard,
Of the unworthiest siege.

That should work. You are very popular in some aspects, and Hamlet may be envious of your special talent.

[handwritten: Laerty wants a role in killing Hamlet]

LAERTES
What part is that, my lord?

What talent is that, my lord?

KING CLAUDIUS
A very riband in the cap of youth,
Yet needful too; for youth no less becomes
The light and careless livery that it wears
Than settled age his sables and his weeds,
Importing health and graveness. Two months since,
Here was a gentleman of Normandy:--
I've seen myself, and served against, the French,
And they can well on horseback: but this gallant
Had witchcraft in't; he grew unto his seat;
And to such wondrous doing brought his horse,
As he had been incorpsed and demi-natured
With the brave beast: so far he topp'd my thought,
That I, in forgery of shapes and tricks,
Come short of what he did.

It's nothing really. But just two months ago, I met a Norman who was a very skillful man on a horse. Even now, I cannot fathom how he did his tricks.

[handwritten: talks of being impressed by a skilled horseman]

LAERTES
A Norman was't?

You say he was a Norman?

KING CLAUDIUS
A Norman.

Yes, a Norman.

LAERTES
Upon my life, Lamond.

I bet it was Lamond.

KING CLAUDIUS
The very same.

Yes, it was.

[handwritten: Is this an allusion of a fictional character?]

LAERTES
I know him well: he is the brooch indeed
And gem of all the nation.

I know him well. He is much loved in his nation.

KING CLAUDIUS
He made confession of you,
And gave you such a masterly report
For art and exercise in your defence
And for your rapier most especially,
That he cried out, 'twould be a sight indeed,
If one could match you: the scrimers of their nation,
He swore, had had neither motion, guard, nor eye,
If you opposed them. Sir, this report of his
Did Hamlet so envenom with his envy
That he could nothing do but wish and beg
Your sudden coming o'er, to play with him.
Now, out of this,--

He said that you were the best swordsman in all of the world. This made Hamlet very envious.

[handwritten: Hamlet jealous of not being called the best]

LAERTES
What out of this, my lord?

What's the poing, my lord?

KING CLAUDIUS
Laertes, was your father dear to you?
Or are you like the painting of a sorrow,
A face without a heart?

Laertes, was your father important to you? Or are you just putting on a show?

LAERTES
Why ask you this?

Asking if Laertes is faking it

Why do you ask this?

KING CLAUDIUS
Not that I think you did not love your father;
But that I know love is begun by time;
And that I see, in passages of proof,
Time qualifies the spark and fire of it.
There lives within the very flame of love
A kind of wick or snuff that will abate it;
And nothing is at a like goodness still;
For goodness, growing to a plurisy,
Dies in his own too much: that we would do
We should do when we would; for this 'would' changes
And hath abatements and delays as many
As there are tongues, are hands, are accidents;
And then this 'should' is like a spendthrift sigh,
That hurts by easing. But, to the quick o' the ulcer:--
Hamlet comes back: what would you undertake,
To show yourself your father's son in deed
More than in words?

It's not that I think you didn't love your father, but I've seen how time changes the love you feel for someone. As the days go by, the fire of love weakens and dies out. We should act when we feel motivated and not wait. My point is Hamlet is coming back. What do you want to do to prove your love for your father.

Convincing him to kill Hamlet

LAERTES
To cut his throat i' the church.

I would cut his throat in the church.

KING CLAUDIUS
No place, indeed, should murder sanctuarize;
Revenge should have no bounds. But, good Laertes,
Will you do this, keep close within your chamber.
Hamlet return'd shall know you are come home:
We'll put on those shall praise your excellence
And set a double varnish on the fame
The Frenchman gave you, bring you in fine together
And wager on your heads: he, being remiss,
Most generous and free from all contriving,
Will not peruse the foils; so that, with ease,
Or with a little shuffling, you may choose
A sword unbated, and in a pass of practise
Requite him for your father.

No one should commit murder in a church. Although revenge has no bounds, I'd like for you to use some restraint. Stay in your room and when Hamlet comes back, we will let him know you are home. We will make much over your abilities the Frenchman mentioned. Then we will bet him he cannot beat you. You will have your chance to take his life and revenge your father.

thinks it's bad to kill someone at church

LAERTES
I will do't:
And, for that purpose, I'll anoint my sword.
I bought an unction of a mountebank,
So mortal that, but dip a knife in it,
Where it draws blood no cataplasm so rare,
Collected from all simples that have virtue
Under the moon, can save the thing from death
That is but scratch'd withal: I'll touch my point
With this contagion, that, if I gall him slightly,
It may be death.

*I will do it.
I will prepare my sword, and I'll poison the tip so if it slightly touches him, he will surely die.*

convinced Hamlet will die

KING CLAUDIUS

Let's further think of this;
Weigh what convenience both of time and means
May fit us to our shape: if this should fail,
And that our drift look through our bad performance,
'Twere better not assay'd: therefore this project
Should have a back or second, that might hold,
If this should blast in proof. Soft! let me see:
We'll make a solemn wager on your cunnings: I ha't.
When in your motion you are hot and dry--
As make your bouts more violent to that end--
And that he calls for drink, I'll have prepared him
A chalice for the nonce, whereon but sipping,
If he by chance escape your venom'd stuck,
Our purpose may hold there.

Let's think about this a little more.
We need to think about the time and place.
We mustn't fail.
If our first plan doesn't work, we need another plan in place. Let me see. You must keep him jumping, so he gets hot and sweaty. Then, when he asks for something to drink, we will have a cup filled with poison prepared for him.

(handwritten: they need to figure out the specifics)

Enter QUEEN GERTRUDE

How now, sweet queen!

What is it, sweet queen?

QUEEN GERTRUDE
One woe doth tread upon another's heel,
So fast they follow; your sister's drown'd, Laertes.

Another tragedy has struck. Your sister has drowned, Laertes.

LAERTES
Drown'd! O, where?

Drowned! Where?

(handwritten: this is very bad news)

QUEEN GERTRUDE
There is a willow grows aslant a brook,
shows his hoar leaves in the glassy stream;
There with fantastic garlands did she come
Of crow-flowers, nettles, daisies, and long purples
That liberal shepherds give a grosser name,
But our cold maids do dead men's fingers call them:
There, on the pendent boughs her coronet weeds
Clambering to hang, an envious sliver broke;
When down her weedy trophies and herself
Fell in the weeping brook. Her clothes spread wide;
And, mermaid-like, awhile they bore her up:
Which time she chanted snatches of old tunes;
As one incapable of her own distress,
Or like a creature native and indued
Unto that element: but long it could not be
Till that her garments, heavy with their drink,
Pull'd the poor wretch from her melodious lay
To muddy death.

There is a willow tree growing by the brook with limbs That stretching over the water. She was there with her flowers when she slipped into the brook. She looked like a mermaid in the water singing her hymns, unaware of the danger she was in. Finally, her drenched clothes, weighed her down.

(handwritten: a very melancholy simile)

LAERTES
Alas, then, she is drown'd?

So, she is dead?

QUEEN GERTRUDE
Drown'd, drown'd.

Drowned.

LAERTES
Too much of water hast thou, poor Ophelia,
And therefore I forbid my tears: but yet
It is our trick; nature her custom holds,

Let shame say what it will: when these are gone,
The woman will be out. Adieu, my lord:
I have a speech of fire, that fain would blaze,
But that this folly douts it.

Ophelia had enough water, so I will not cry anymore. Nature is too strong and makes me cry anyway. When I am finished, I will not act like a woman. Goodbye, my lord. I have more fiery

words to say, but my tears won't let me.

(handwritten: that is very strong to not cry)

(handwritten page note)

108

Exit

KING CLAUDIUS
Let's follow, Gertrude:
How much I had to do to calm his rage!
Now fear I this will give it start again;
Therefore let's follow.

Exeunt

Let's follow him, Gertrude. I have worked so hard to calm him down and I'm afraid this might start him up again. So, let's follow him.

his hard
work was ruined
by the news

Act V

Scene I

A churchyard

Enter two Clowns, with spades, & c

First Clown
Is she to be buried in Christian burial that
wilfully seeks her own salvation?

Are they going to give her a Christian burial to try and save her after she did the unforgivable.

Is this referring to Ophelia?

Second Clown
I tell thee she is: and therefore make her grave
straight: the crowner hath sat on her, and finds it
Christian burial.

I'm telling you they are; therefore, maker her grave straight. The coroner has said it was an accident.

First Clown
How can that be, unless she drowned herself in her own
defence?

How can that be? Did she drown herself in self-defense?

Second Clown
Why, 'tis found so.

I guess so.

First Clown
It must be 'se offendendo;' it cannot be else.
For here lies the point: if I drown myself wittingly,
it argues an act: and an act hath three branches: it
is, to act, to do, to perform: argal, she drowned
herself wittingly.

I think she knew what she was doing. She acted on her own wits.

Yes, refers to her act of suicide

Second Clown
Nay, but hear you, goodman delver,--

No, listen to me, gravedigger.

First Clown
Give me leave. Here lies the water; good:
here stands the man; good; if the man go to this water,
and drown himself, it is, will he, nill he, he goes,
--mark you that; but if the water come to him
and drown him, he drowns not himself: argal, he
that is not guilty of his own death shortens not his own life.

Just let me finish. Here is the water, right? Here is the man. If the man goes into the water and drowns himself it is his will. If the water comes to him, then it is an accident. If you don't mean to kill yourself, then you can receive salvation.

Second Clown
But is this law?

Is that the law?

First Clown
Ay, marry, is't; crowner's quest law.

Yes, it is the law of the coroner.

Second Clown
Will you ha' the truth on't? If this had not been
a gentlewoman, she should have been buried out o'
Christian burial.

I think if she hadn't been wealthy, she would not have received a Christian burial.

First Clown
Why, there thou say'st: and the more pity that
great folk should have countenance in this world to
drown or hang themselves, more than their even
Christian. Come, my spade. There is no ancient
gentleman but gardeners, ditchers, and grave-makers:
they hold up Adam's profession.

Isn't that a shame. Great people are poor, like gardeners, ditch-diggers, and gravediggers. Yet, they have the same profession as Adam.

her money got her a burial

Second Clown
Was he a gentleman?

Was he a great man.

First Clown
He was the first that ever bore arms.

He was the first man with arms.

Second Clown
Why, he had none.

Didn't he have any?

First Clown
What, art a heathen? How dost thou understand the
Scripture? The Scripture says 'Adam digged:' could
he dig without arms? I'll put another question to thee:
if thou answerest me not to the purpose, confess thyself--

Are you a heathen. Don't you read the scripture? It says, "Adam dug." He could not do this without arms. Let me ask you something.

Second Clown
Go to.

Go ahead.

very religious clown

First Clown
What is he that builds stronger than either the mason,
the shipwright, or the carpenter?

Who can build stronger than a mason, a ship builder, or a carpenter?

Second Clown
The gallows-maker; for that frame outlives a thousand
tenants.

The man who builds gallows. His work outlives many who use it.

First Clown
I like thy wit well, in good faith: the gallows
does well; but how does it well? it does well to
those that do in: now thou dost ill to say the
gallows is built stronger than the church: argal,
the gallows may do well to thee. To't again, come.

That's rather smart. You think the gallows are stronger than the church.

Second Clown
'Who builds stronger than a mason, a shipwright, or a
carpenter?'

Who builds stronger than a mason, a ship builder, or a carpenter.

Interesting topic of conversation

First Clown
Ay, tell me that, and unyoke.

Yes. Tell me what you think.

Second Clown
Marry, now I can tell.

I've got it.

First Clown
To't.

Go ahead.

Second Clown
Mass, I cannot tell.

I swear. I can't think.

Enter HAMLET and HORATIO, at a distance

First Clown
Cudgel thy brains no more about it, for your dull
ass will not mend his pace with beating; and, when
you are asked this question next, say 'a
grave-maker: 'the houses that he makes last till
doomsday. Go, get thee to Yaughan: fetch me a
stoup of liquor.

Don't overthink it. You are dumb to get it. The gravedigger is the greatest builder, because what he builds lasts until the end of time. Now, go and get me some liquor.

that is a profound statement

Exit Second Clown

He digs and sings

In youth, when I did love, did love,
Methought it was very sweet,
To contract, O, the time, for, ah, my behove,
O, methought, there was nothing meet.

*When I was younger, I did love, did love.
I thought it was very sweet. To set the day and time for us to meet.*

HAMLET
Has this fellow no feeling of his business, that he sings at grave-making?

Does this guy have no respect for the dead; he is singing while digging a grave.

[handwritten: another interesting song]

HORATIO
Custom hath made it in him a property of easiness.

He is just numb to his work after doing it for so long.

HAMLET
'Tis e'en so: the hand of little employment hath the daintier sense.

I agree. He has so much to do, he can't afford to be sensitive.

First Clown
[Sings]
But age, with his stealing steps,
Hath claw'd me in his clutch,
And hath shipped me intil the land,
As if I had never been such.

Old age has snuck up on me, and got me in his clutches. He slipped into the land, as if I never existed.

[handwritten: can't feel much emotion given his job]

Throws up a skull

HAMLET
That skull had a tongue in it, and could sing once:
how the knave jowls it to the ground, as if it were
Cain's jaw-bone, that did the first murder!
It might be the pate of a politician, which this ass
now o'er-reaches; one that would circumvent God,
might it not?

That skull once had a tongue in it and could sing. Now that fool tosses it to the ground as if it belonged to a murderer! It might have belonged to a silver-tongued politician, and now this guy is overthrowing him. Right?

[handwritten: a very sad line]

HORATIO
It might, my lord.

It might have been.

HAMLET
Or of a courtier; which could say 'Good morrow,
sweet lord! How dost thou, good lord?'
This might be my lord such-a-one, that praised my lord
such-a-one's horse, when he meant to beg it; might it not?

Or it could have been a courtier who said, "Good morning, sweet lord! How are you?" Couldn't it?

HORATIO
Ay, my lord.

Yes, my lord.

HAMLET
Why, e'en so: and now my Lady Worm's; chapless, and
knocked about the mazzard with a sexton's spade:
here's fine revolution, an we had the trick to
see't. Did these bones cost no more the breeding,
but to play at loggats with 'em? mine ache to think on't.

Even if that's true, it now belongs to Lady Worm. He has been knocked around with a shovel. It is worthless now. It makes me ache to think about it.

First Clown
[Sings]
A pick-axe, and a spade, a spade,
For and a shrouding sheet:
O, a pit of clay for to be made
For such a guest is meet.

[handwritten: Personification of the worm]

A pick-ax and a shovel for a dead man's burial clothes with a bed of clay.

Throws up another skull

HAMLET

There's another: why may not that be the skull of a lawyer? Where be his quiddities now, his quillets, his cases, his tenures, and his tricks? why does he suffer this rude knave now to knock him about the sconce with a dirty shovel, and will not tell him of his action of battery? Hum! This fellow might be in's time a great buyer of land, with his statutes, his recognizances, his fines, his double vouchers, his recoveries: is this the fine of his fines, and the recovery of his recoveries, to have his fine pate full of fine dirt? will his vouchers vouch him no more of his purchases, and double ones too, than the length and breadth of a pair of indentures? The very conveyances of his lands will hardly lie in this box; and must the inheritor himself have no more, ha?

There goes another one. Maybe that one is a lawyer. Where are his tricks and fees, now? Why does he let this guy treat him like this? Or, it could be a great land owner with his lumps of money and renter's fees. Is this the fine for him, having his skull filled with dirt? The only thing he has to his name is his coffin.

reflecting on significance of life and death

HORATIO

Not a jot more, my lord.

Not much more, my lord.

HAMLET

Is not parchment made of sheepskins?

Isn't paper made of sheepskins?

HORATIO

Ay, my lord, and of calf-skins too.

Yes, my lord, and calf-skins, too.

HAMLET

They are sheep and calves which seek out assurance in that. I will speak to this fellow. Whose grave's this, sirrah?

Only sheep and calves have assurance of their purpose after death. I am going to speak to this guy. Whose grave is this, sir?

First Clown

Mine, sir.

Mine, sir.

Sings

once again very profound

O, a pit of clay for to be made
For such a guest is meet.

Oh, a pit of clay to be made for the dead to meet.

HAMLET

I think it be thine, indeed; for thou liest in't.

You'll think it's yours when you're lying in it.

First Clown

You lie out on't, sir, and therefore it is not yours: for my part, I do not lie in't, and yet it is mine.

You may lay in it, sir, but it would not be yours; however, I don't lay in it and it is mine.

HAMLET

'Thou dost lie in't, to be in't and say it is thine: 'tis for the dead, not for the quick; therefore thou liest.

One must lay in it for it to be theirs. It is for the dead, not the living, you liar.

First Clown

'Tis a quick lie, sir; 'twill away gain, from me to you.

It's just a little lie, sir.

HAMLET

What man dost thou dig it for?

What man do you dig it for?

graves are for the dead only

First Clown

For no man, sir.

It is not for a man.

HAMLET
What woman, then?

What women, then?

First Clown
For none, neither.

None.

HAMLET
Who is to be buried in't?

Who is to be buried in it?

First Clown
One that was a woman, sir; but, rest her soul, she's dead.

Well, she was a woman, but now she is dead.

HAMLET
How absolute the knave is! we must speak by the card, or equivocation will undo us. By the Lord, Horatio, these three years I have taken a note of it; the age is grown so picked that the toe of the peasant comes so near the heel of the courtier, he gaffs his kibe. How long hast thou been a grave-maker?

lose identity once you pass away

How simple-minded this fool is! We must be so specific or he doesn't get it. I swear, Horatio, there is a fine line between the peasants and the educated. How long have you been a gravedigger?

First Clown
Of all the days i' the year, I came to't that day that our last king Hamlet overcame Fortinbras.

I became a gravedigger the day the late King Hamlet defeated Fortinbras.

HAMLET
How long is that since?

How long has that been?

First Clown
Cannot you tell that? every fool can tell that: it was the very day that young Hamlet was born; he thatis mad, and sent into England.

Don't you know that? Every fool knows that day; the day young Hamlet, the one who went mad and was sent to England, was born.

HAMLET
Ay, marry, why was he sent into England? *did not*

Oh yes, and why was he sent to England?

First Clown
Why, because he was mad: he shall recover his wits there; *know it was* or, if he do not, it's no great matter there. *Hamlet?*

I think it was because he was mad, and needed some time to regain his senses. If he doesn't it does not matter.

HAMLET
Why?

Why?

First Clown
'Twill, a not be seen in him there; there the men are as mad as he.

Because there, no one will notice.

HAMLET
How came he mad?

Why did he go crazy?

First Clown
Very strangely, they say.

People say it was very strange?

HAMLET
How strangely?

the story has some holes

How so?

First Clown
Faith, e'en with losing his wits.

He lost his mind.

HAMLET
Upon what ground?

On what grounds?

First Clown
Why, here in Denmark:
I have been sexton here, man and boy, thirty years.

Here in Denmark.
I have lived here the past thirty years.

HAMLET
How long will a man lie i' the earth ere he rot?

How long does it take a man to rot once he is buried?

First Clown
I' faith, if he be not rotten before he die--as we
have many pocky corses now-a-days, that will scarce
hold the laying in--he will last you some eight year
or nine year: a tanner will last you nine year.

If he is not rotten before he dies, and we see that a lot these
days, he will last eight or nine years. A leather-maker will last at
least nine years.

[handwritten: many rot prior to death]

HAMLET
Why he more than another?

Why does he last longer?

First Clown
Why, sir, his hide is so tanned with his trade, that
he will keep out water a great while; and your water
is a sore decayer of your whoreson dead body.
Here's a skull now; this skull has lain in the earth
three and twenty years.

Because his skin is so tough from his line of work, it keeps the
water out. Water is what decays the body. This skull here has
been in the earth twenty-three years.

HAMLET
Whose was it?

Whose was it?

First Clown
A whoreson mad fellow's it was: whose do you think it was?

Some crazy guy. Who do you think it was?

HAMLET
Nay, I know not.

I don't know.

First Clown
A pestilence on him for a mad rogue! a' poured a
flagon of Rhenish on my head once. This same skull,
sir, was Yorick's skull, the king's jester.

This guy was a crazy pest! He poured a whole bottle of wine on
my head once. This, sir, was Yorick, the kin's jester.

HAMLET
This?

This?

First Clown
E'en that.

Yes, that.

HAMLET
Let me see.

Let me see.

Takes the skull

[handwritten: way connected with the person of the grave]

Alas, poor Yorick! I knew him, Horatio: a fellow
of infinite jest, of most excellent fancy: he hath
borne me on his back a thousand times; and now, how
abhorred in my imagination it is! my gorge rims at it.
Here hung those lips that I have kissed I know
not how oft. Where be your gibes now? your
gambols? your songs? your flashes of merriment,
that were wont to set the table on a roar? Not one
now, to mock your own grinning? quite chap-fallen?
Now get you to my lady's chamber, and tell her, let
her paint an inch thick, to this favour she must
come; make her laugh at that. Prithee, Horatio, tell

Oh, poor Yorick! I knew him, Horatio. He was a funny fellow.
He rode me on his back a thousand times. This is terrible and
makes me sick. Here is where his lips, I kissed, used to be.
Where are your jokes, now? Your songs? Your humor that used
to make everyone laugh? Now, go to my lady's room and tell her
she is going to end up like you someday. That'll make her laugh.
Tell me one thing, Horatio.

[handwritten: Hamlet knew him too]

me one thing.

HORATIO
What's that, my lord?

HAMLET
Dost thou think Alexander looked o' this fashion i'
the earth?

HORATIO
E'en so.

HAMLET
And smelt so? pah!

Puts down the skull

HORATIO
E'en so, my lord.

HAMLET
To what base uses we may return, Horatio!
Why may not imagination trace the noble dust of Alexander,
till he find it stopping a bung-hole?

HORATIO
'Twere to consider too curiously, to consider so.

HAMLET
No, faith, not a jot; but to follow him thither with
modesty enough, and likelihood to lead it:
thus: Alexander died, Alexander was buried,
Alexander returneth into dust; the dust is earth;
of earth we make loam; and why of that loam,
whereto he was converted, might they not stop a
beer-barrel?
Imperious Caesar, dead and turn'd to clay,
Might stop a hole to keep the wind away:
O, that that earth, which kept the world in awe,
Should patch a wall to expel the winter flaw!
But soft! but soft! aside: here comes the king.

Enter Priest, & c. in procession; the Corpse of OPHELIA, LAERTES and Mourners following; KING CLAUDIUS, QUEEN GERTRUDE, their trains, & c

The queen, the courtiers: who is this they follow?
And with such maimed rites? This doth betoken
The corse they follow did with desperate hand
Fordo its own life: 'twas of some estate.
Couch we awhile, and mark.

Retiring with HORATIO

LAERTES
What ceremony else?

HAMLET
That is Laertes,
A very noble youth: mark.

What's that, my lord?

*Do you think Alexander the Great looked like this when
he was buried?*

Probably so.

And smelled this bad? Whew!

Yes, my lord.

*It's horrible what happens to us in the end, Horatio!
Can you believe the noble dust of Alexander the Great could end
up as a plug?*

It's hard to imagine.

*No, not really. Follow me: First he died and was buried. Then
he returns to the dust which is basically the earth. The earth
creates loam and the loam is used to plug a beer barrel. Ceasar,
died and was turned into clay. He might stop a hole to keep out
the wind. Oh, to think the once great man now plugs up a wall.
But, wait! Be quiet! Here comes the king.*

*Who are the queen and her courtiers following? And with such
somber ceremony. This means the corpse took its own life. Must
be from a wealthy fellow. Let's stay and watch a while.*

What ceremony are you going to preach?

Look. That is Laertes, a very noble young man.

Allusion to Alexander the Great

Hamlet is currently in a bad place

Same allusion with Caesar

Is Hamlet unaware of Ophelia's death?

LAERTES
What ceremony else?

What ceremony are you going to preach?

First Priest
Her obsequies have been as far enlarged
As we have warrantise: her death was doubtful;
And, but that great command o'ersways the order,
She should in ground unsanctified have lodged
Till the last trumpet: for charitable prayers,
Shards, flints and pebbles should be thrown on her;
Yet here she is allow'd her virgin crants,
Her maiden strewments and the bringing home
Of bell and burial.

I've said as much as I can, since her death was suspicious. She should be buried outside the church graveyard, and have stones thrown onto her grave. Instead, she is here, buried in sacred ground, dressed like a virgin with flowers all around and the tolling of the bells.

Priest finds her death oddly suspicious

LAERTES
Must there no more be done?

Isn't there anything else that can be done?

First Priest
No more be done:
We should profane the service of the dead
To sing a requiem and such rest to her
As to peace-parted souls.

No more can be done. It would be disrespectful to the other dead if we gave her any more rites.

LAERTES
Lay her i' the earth:
And from her fair and unpolluted flesh
May violets spring! I tell thee, churlish priest,
A ministering angel shall my sister be,
When thou liest howling.

cant offend the rest of the dead

Go ahead then, and lay her in the ground. May violets grow from her grave. I tell you priest, my sister will be an angel in heaven while you're howling in hell.

HAMLET
What, the fair Ophelia!

What? The beautiful Ophelia!

QUEEN GERTRUDE
Sweets to the sweet: farewell!

Flowers for the sweet. Goodbye!

Scattering flowers

I hoped thou shouldst have been my Hamlet's wife;
I thought thy bride-bed to have deck'd, sweet maid,
And not have strew'd thy grave.

I had hoped you would be my daughter-in-law. I rather be decorating your bridal bed than your grave, sweet girl.

LAERTES
O, treble woe
Fall ten times treble on that cursed head,
Whose wicked deed thy most ingenious sense
Deprived thee of! Hold off the earth awhile,
Till I have caught her once more in mine arms:

Gertrude clearly loved her aswell

Oh, my troubles. May curses fall ten times on the head who cause this. Wait! Let me hold her once more!

Leaps into the grave

Now pile your dust upon the quick and dead,
Till of this flat a mountain you have made,
To o'ertop old Pelion, or the skyish head
Of blue Olympus.

Now throw the dirt on both of us until you have made a mountain.

HAMLET
[Advancing]
What is he whose grief
Bears such an emphasis? whose phrase of sorrow
Conjures the wandering stars, and makes them stand

Who is the one whose grief is so loud and whose words are so sad the stars stand still. It is me, Hamlet the Dane.

love that reference

Like wonder-wounded hearers? This is I,
Hamlet the Dane.

Leaps into the grave

LAERTES
The devil take thy soul!

May the devil take your soul!

Grappling with him

HAMLET
Thou pray'st not well.
I prithee, take thy fingers from my throat;
For, though I am not splenitive and rash,
Yet have I something in me dangerous,
Which let thy wiseness fear: hold off thy hand.

You don't know how to pray. Take your fingers from my throat.
Be smart, and do not make me angry. Take your hands off of me.

KING CLAUDIUS
Pluck them asunder.

Pull them out.

QUEEN GERTRUDE
Hamlet, Hamlet!

Hamlet, Hamlet!

All
Gentlemen,--

Gentlemen...

HORATIO
Good my lord, be quiet.

Good my lord, be quiet.

The Attendants part them, and they come out of the grave

HAMLET
Why I will fight with him upon this theme
Until my eyelids will no longer wag.

I will fight him over this until my eyes are permanently closed.

QUEEN GERTRUDE
O my son, what theme?

Oh my son, what are fighting for?

HAMLET
I loved Ophelia: forty thousand brothers
Could not, with all their quantity of love,
Make up my sum. What wilt thou do for her?

I loved Ophelia. Forty thousand brothers could not have loved
her more. What are you going to do for her?

KING CLAUDIUS
O, he is mad, Laertes.

Oh, he is crazy, Laertes.

QUEEN GERTRUDE
For love of God, forbear him.

For the love of God don't listen to him.

HAMLET
'Swounds, show me what thou'lt do:
Woo't weep? woo't fight? woo't fast? woo't tear thyself?
Woo't drink up eisel? eat a crocodile?
I'll do't. Dost thou come here to whine?
To outface me with leaping in her grave?
Be buried quick with her, and so will I:
And, if thou prate of mountains, let them throw
Millions of acres on us, till our ground,
Singeing his pate against the burning zone,
Make Ossa like a wart! Nay, an thou'lt mouth,
I'll rant as well as thou.

Show me what you are going to do. Will you cry? Will you fight?
Will you fast? Will you tear at your skin? Will you drink bile?
Eat a crocodile? I'll do all of that. Did you come here to cry and
whine? To outdo me by jumping in her grave. To be buried with
her? So, will I. You want them to over us with dirt. Let them
make mountains over us. See, I can talk as well as you.

[handwritten: an interesting situation]

[handwritten: Hamlet is very get on fighting him]

[handwritten: he would do anything for her love]

QUEEN GERTRUDE
This is mere madness:
And thus awhile the fit will work on him;
Anon, as patient as the female dove,
When that her golden couplets are disclosed,
His silence will sit drooping.

This is crazy.
He will be like this for a while. It will pass and he will be as peaceful as a dove.

HAMLET
Hear you, sir;
What is the reason that you use me thus?
I loved you ever: but it is no matter;
Let Hercules himself do what he may,
The cat will mew and dog will have his day.

Hamlet never disrespected Laertes

Listen to me, sir.
Why are you acting towards me like this? I've always loved you. But, it doesn't matter. Even Hercules can't make change the way a cat or dog acts.

Exit

KING CLAUDIUS
I pray you, good Horatio, wait upon him.

Please, Horatio, get him out of here.

Exit HORATIO

To LAERTES

Strengthen your patience in our last night's speech;
We'll put the matter to the present push.
Good Gertrude, set some watch over your son.
This grave shall have a living monument:
An hour of quiet shortly shall we see;
Till then, in patience our proceeding be.

Remember what we talked about last night and be patient. We'll put this matter to rest soon. Gertrude, get someone to watch over your son. We will build a monument to put on this grave. Now, we have the quiet we need, so please proceed.

Exeunt

they still want to kill Hamlet

Scene II

A hall in the castle

Enter HAMLET and HORATIO

HAMLET
So much for this, sir: now shall you see the other;
You do remember all the circumstance?

That's enough about that, sir. Let me tell you about what happened. You remember what was going on you.

HORATIO
Remember it, my lord?

Remember, my lord?

HAMLET
Sir, in my heart there was a kind of fighting,
That would not let me sleep: methought I lay
Worse than the mutines in the bilboes. Rashly,
And praised be rashness for it, let us know,
Our indiscretion sometimes serves us well,
When our deep plots do pall: and that should teach us
There's a divinity that shapes our ends,
Rough-hew them how we will,--

Sir, I was in constant turmoil, and I couldn't sleep. It was worse than being a prisoner. I acted crazily and hastily, but my plans were stalled. God's will always prevails, no matter how far we stray.

HORATIO
That is most certain.

That's for sure.

despite the time, whats meant to happen will happen

HAMLET
Up from my cabin,
My sea-gown scarf'd about me, in the dark
Groped I to find out them; had my desire.
Finger'd their packet, and in fine withdrew
To mine own room again; making so bold,
My fears forgetting manners, to unseal
Their grand commission; where I found, Horatio,--
O royal knavery!--an exact command,
Larded with many several sorts of reasons
Importing Denmark's health and England's too,
With, ho! such bugs and goblins in my life,
That, on the supervise, no leisure bated,
No, not to stay the grinding of the axe,
My head should be struck off.

When I was out to sea, I came up from my cabin and looked around in the dark. I found papers, which I took back to my own room, and discovered the King had ordered my death.

HORATIO
Is't possible?

Claudius to kill Hamlet

Are you serious?

HAMLET
Here's the commission: read it at more leisure.
But wilt thou hear me how I did proceed?

Here's the letter. Read it for yourself. But, let me tell you the rest.

HORATIO
I beseech you.

Please.

HAMLET
Being thus be-netted round with villanies,--
Ere I could make a prologue to my brains,
They had begun the play--I sat me down,
Devised a new commission, wrote it fair:
I once did hold it, as our statists do,

*There I was trapped. So, I wrote a new commission.
My education came in handy for I wrote like a diplomat. Do you want to know what I wrote?*

complimenting himself

A baseness to write fair and labour'd much
How to forget that learning, but, sir, now
It did me yeoman's service: wilt thou know
The effect of what I wrote?

HORATIO
Ay, good my lord.

Yes, of course, my lord.

HAMLET
An earnest conjuration from the king,
As England was his faithful tributary,
As love between them like the palm might flourish,
As peace should stiff her wheaten garland wear
And stand a comma 'tween their amities,
And many such-like 'As'es of great charge,
That, on the view and knowing of these contents,
Without debatement further, more or less,
He should the bearers put to sudden death,
Not shriving-time allow'd.

I wrote an earnest plea from the King, with a lot of crap about the relationship between England and Denmark. I asked that the men delivering the letter be put to death without confession to a priest.

HORATIO
How was this seal'd?

very interesting

How did you seal the letter?

HAMLET
Why, even in that was heaven ordinant.
I had my father's signet in my purse,
Which was the model of that Danish seal;
Folded the writ up in form of the other,
Subscribed it, gave't the impression, placed it safely,
The changeling never known. Now, the next day
Was our sea-fight; and what to this was sequent
Thou know'st already.

Even God's hand was in that as well. I had my father's signet ring with me, so I used it to seal the letter. Then, I exchanged the letters. The next day our ship was attacked, and you know the rest.

that was the letter to Horatio

HORATIO
So Guildenstern and Rosencrantz go to't.

So Guildenstern and Rosencrantz are in big trouble.

HAMLET
Why, man, they did make love to this employment;
They are not near my conscience; their defeat
Does by their own insinuation grow:
'Tis dangerous when the baser nature comes
Between the pass and fell incensed points
Of mighty opposites.

Yes, they are and it's their own fault. They were just commoners caught in a fight between two powerful men.

HORATIO
Why, what a king is this!

What a king Claudius is!

HAMLET
Does it not, think'st thee, stand me now upon--
He that hath kill'd my king and whored my mother,
Popp'd in between the election and my hopes,
Thrown out his angle for my proper life,
And with such cozenage--is't not perfect conscience,
To quit him with this arm? and is't not to be damn'd,
To let this canker of our nature come
In further evil?

Don't you think it is time for me to kill the king, who killed my father and made my mother a whore? Isn't it time to put an end to him with my sword, and without damage to my conscience. And, wouldn't I be at fault if I let this devil continue to bring evil to our country?

wants the insight from Horatio

HORATIO
It must be shortly known to him from England
What is the issue of the business there.

He's going to find out soon what happened in England.

HAMLET
It will be short: the interim is mine;
And a man's life's no more than to say 'One.'
But I am very sorry, good Horatio,
That to Laertes I forgot myself;
For, by the image of my cause, I see
The portraiture of his: I'll court his favours.
But, sure, the bravery of his grief did put me
Into a towering passion.

It will be soon, but I have some time.
I am very sorry, Horatio, for what I did to Laertes.
I lost control when I saw his overplayed grief. His situation is
very much like mine, and I am going to be nice to him.

remorse

with actions

towards

Laertes

HORATIO
Peace! who comes here?

Wait! Who's there?

Enter OSRIC

OSRIC
Your lordship is right welcome back to Denmark.

Welcome back to Denmark, my lord.

HAMLET
I humbly thank you, sir. Dost know this water-fly?

Thank you, sir. Do you know this fellow?

HORATIO
No, my good lord.

No, my lord.

HAMLET
Thy state is the more gracious; for 'tis a vice to
know him. He hath much land, and fertile: let a
beast be lord of beasts, and his crib shall stand at
the king's mess: 'tis a chough; but, as I say,
spacious in the possession of dirt.

You're lucky. He's a great land owner, but he is a beast.
He is treated well because he is wealthy.

New landowner
is
introduced

OSRIC
Sweet lord, if your lordship were at leisure,
I should impart a thing to you from his majesty.

My lord, if you have a minute, I have a message from the king.

HAMLET
I will receive it, sir, with all diligence of spirit.
Put your bonnet to his right use; 'tis for the head.

Go ahead, sir. I will listen in rapture, but put your hat back on.

OSRIC
I thank your lordship, it is very hot.

Thank you, lord, it is very hot.

HAMLET
No, believe me, 'tis very cold; the wind is northerly.

No, believe me, it's very cold. The wind is blowing from the
north.

OSRIC
It is indifferent cold, my lord, indeed.

Yes, I think it is cold.

HAMLET
But yet methinks it is very sultry and hot for my complexion.

Yet, I think the air is hot and humid, which is bad for my skin.

OSRIC
Exceedingly, my lord; it is very sultry,--as 'twere,
I cannot tell how.
But, my lord, hismajesty bade me signify to you that he has
laid agreat wager on your head: sir, this is the matter,--

Right, my lord, it is humid. But, my lord, the king wants you to --
know he has placed a large wager on you. This is the deal...

a
very
obedient
man

HAMLET
I beseech you, remember--

Please, go on...

HAMLET moves him to put on his hat

OSRIC
Nay, good my lord; for mine ease, in good faith.
Sir, here is newly come to court Laertes; believe
me, an absolute gentleman, full of most excellent
differences, of very soft society and great showing:
indeed, to speak feelingly of him, he is the card or
calendar of gentry, for you shall find in him the
continent of what part a gentleman would see.

No, my lord, I'm fine, I swear.
Laertes has come back. He is a great gentleman and very
popular in society. If I may speak freely, I think he is the object
of what a gentleman should be.

[handwritten: → that might be a bad idea]

HAMLET
Sir, his definement suffers no perdition in you;
finer though, I know, to divide him inventorially would
doubt you dizzy the arithmetic of memory, and yet but yaw
neither, in respect of his quick sail. But, in the
verity of extolment, I take him to be a soul of
great article; and his infusion of such dearth and
rareness, as, to make true diction of him, his
semblable is his mirror; and who else would trace
him, his umbrage, nothing more.

Sir, I see you think very highly of him; you don't have to list his
qualities. I don't even think you could break them all down. I
can find a man as good as he.

OSRIC
Your lordship speaks most infallibly of him.

You are right, my lord.

HAMLET
The concernancy, sir? why do we wrap the gentleman
in our more rawer breath?

Anyway, why are we talking about him?

[handwritten: ↓ Hamlet is confused]

OSRIC
Sir?

What, sir?

HORATIO
Is't not possible to understand in another tongue?
You will do't, sir, really.

Try it again.

HAMLET
What imports the nomination of this gentleman?

What is the significance of us talking about him?

OSRIC
Of Laertes?

You mean Laertes?

HORATIO
His purse is empty already; all's golden words are spent.

His ability to comprehend has vanished.

HAMLET
Of him, sir.

Yes, sir. Laertes.

[handwritten: ↓ did osric just forget?]

OSRIC
I know you are not ignorant--

I know you know Laertes...

HAMLET
I would you did, sir; yet, in faith, if you did,
it would not much approve me. Well, sir?

I know him well enough. So...

OSRIC
You are not ignorant of what excellence Laertes is--

Then you must know how excellent Laertes is...

HAMLET
I dare not confess that, lest I should compare with
him in excellence; but, to know a man well, were to
know himself.

I wouldn't say I know what you are getting at.

[handwritten: → Interesting point]

OSRIC
I mean, sir, for his weapon;
but in the imputation laid on him by them,
 in his meed he's unfellowed.

I mean his known for his ability in fencing.
No one is as good as he.

HAMLET
What's his weapon?

What is his weapon?

Will this make Hamlet jealous?

OSRIC
Rapier and dagger.

The rapier and the dagger.

HAMLET
That's two of his weapons: but, well.

Okay, that's two; go on.

OSRIC
The king, sir, hath wagered with him six Barbary
horses: against the which he has imponed, as I take
it, six French rapiers and poniards, with their
assigns, as girdle, hangers, and so: three of the
carriages, in faith, are very dear to fancy, very
responsive to the hilts, most delicate carriages,
and of very liberal conceit.

The king, sir, has bet him six of his finest horses and six rapiers
and dagger with their carriages.

Is this the bet they were talking about

HAMLET
What call you the carriages?

What are carriages?

HORATIO
I knew you must be edified by the margent ere you had
done.

I knew you were going to be stumped before we were done.

OSRIC
The carriages, sir, are the hangers.

The carriages are the sheaths to put the swords in.

HAMLET
The phrase would be more german to the matter, if we
could carry cannon by our sides: I would it might
be hangers till then. But, on. six Barbary horses
against six French swords, their assigns, and three
liberal-conceited carriages; that's the French bet
against the Danish. Why is this 'imponed,' as you call it?

I would not use the word carriage. It sounds like you are
carrying a canon on your side. I'll call it a hanger. However,
that is a mighty steep bet. What is the bet upon?

OSRIC
The king, sir, hath laid, that in a dozen passes
between yourself and him, he shall not exceed you
three hits: he hath laid on twelve for nine; and it
would come to immediate trial, if your lordship
would vouchsafe the answer.

The king, sir, has bet that Laertes cannot beat you by three hits
in a dozen rounds. If you'll accept, we can start right away.

their plan seems to be working

HAMLET
How if I answer 'no'?

What if I say no?

OSRIC
I mean, my lord, the opposition of your person in trial.

You should tell them yourself.

HAMLET
Sir, I will walk here in the hall: if it please his
majesty, 'tis the breathing time of day with me; let
the foils be brought, the gentleman willing, and the
king hold his purpose, I will win for him an I can;
if not, I will gain nothing but my shame and the odd hits.

Sir, I will walk here in the hall, and if it pleases the king, he can
bring on the gentleman. I will do what I can to win the bet. If I
don't, then I will only be slightly embarrassed.

OSRIC
Shall I re-deliver you e'en so?

Shall I go tell them what you said?

HAMLET
To this effect, sir; after what flourish your nature will.

Certainly, tell them whatever you want.

OSRIC
I commend my duty to your lordship.

I am at your service.

HAMLET
Yours, yours.

And I am at yours.

Exit OSRIC

pretty kind to Osric

He does well to commend it himself;
there are no tongues else for's turn.

He must commend his service, himself, because no one else will.

HORATIO
This lapwing runs away with the shell on his head.

He is kind of nutty.

HAMLET
He did comply with his dug, before he sucked it.
Thus has he--and many more of the same bevy that I
know the dressy age dotes on--only got the tune of
the time and outward habit of encounter; a kind of
yesty collection, which carries them through and
through the most fond and winnowed opinions; and do
but blow them to their trial, the bubbles are out.

*Yes, but he has gathered enough around here to get him by. But,
he still is what he is.*

Enter a Lord

he is pretty well off

Lord
My lord, his majesty commended him to you by young
Osric, who brings back to him that you attend him in
the hall: he sends to know if your pleasure hold to
play with Laertes, or that you will take longer time.

*My lord, the king has talked with Osric and wants to know if you
are ready or if you need more time.*

HAMLET
I am constant to my purpose; they follow the king's
pleasure: if his fitness speaks, mine is ready; now
or whensoever, provided I be so able as now.

Whenever.

Lord
The king and queen and all are coming down.

he has

The king and queen are coming.

HAMLET
In happy time.

all the time

In their own sweet time.

in the world

Lord
The queen desires you to use some gentle
entertainment to Laertes before you fall to play.

The queen wants you to speak with Laertes before you begin.

HAMLET
She well instructs me.

She always has some instructions for me.

Exit Lord

HORATIO
You will lose this wager, my lord.

You will lose this wager, my lord.

HAMLET

Horatio is convined

126

I do not think so: since he went into France, I
have been in continual practise:
I shall win at the odds.
But thou wouldst not think how ill all's here about my heart:
but it is no matter.

HORATIO
Nay, good my lord,--

HAMLET
It is but foolery; but it is such a kind of
gain-giving, as would perhaps trouble a woman.

HORATIO
If your mind dislike any thing, obey it:
I will forestall their repair hither, and say you are not fit.

HAMLET
Not a whit, we defy augury: there's a special
providence in the fall of a sparrow. If it be now,
'tis not to come; if it be not to come, it will be
now; if it be not now, yet it will come: the
readiness is all: since no man has aught of what he
leaves, what is't to leave betimes?

Enter KING CLAUDIUS, QUEEN GERTRUDE, LAERTES, Lords, OSRIC, and Attendants with foils, & c

KING CLAUDIUS
Come, Hamlet, come, and take this hand from me.

KING CLAUDIUS puts LAERTES' hand into HAMLET's

HAMLET
Give me your pardon, sir: I've done you wrong;
But pardon't, as you are a gentleman.
This presence knows,
And you must needs have heard, how I am punish'd
With sore distraction. What I have done,
That might your nature, honour and exception
Roughly awake, I here proclaim was madness.
Was't Hamlet wrong'd Laertes? Never Hamlet:
If Hamlet from himself be ta'en away,
And when he's not himself does wrong Laertes,
Then Hamlet does it not, Hamlet denies it.
Who does it, then? His madness: if't be so,
Hamlet is of the faction that is wrong'd;
His madness is poor Hamlet's enemy.
Sir, in this audience,
Let my disclaiming from a purposed evil
Free me so far in your most generous thoughts,
That I have shot mine arrow o'er the house,
And hurt my brother.

LAERTES
I am satisfied in nature,
Whose motive, in this case, should stir me most
To my revenge: but in my terms of honour
I stand aloof; and will no reconcilement,
Till by some elder masters, of known honour,
I have a voice and precedent of peace,
To keep my name ungored. But till that time,

I don't think so. I've been practicing since he went to France.

The odds are in my favor, but I still feel something is not quite right. Oh, well.

This is not a good idea...

I know it's foolish.

If you feel like something is not right, just say the word, and I'll stop the match.

No way! I don't put a lot of faith in superstitions. If it's God's will, then so be it.

Come Hamlet and shake hands.

Forgive me, sir. I've done you wrong. I'm afraid I was crazy. If I were in my right mind, I would have never committed such a heinous act. My madness is my true enemy. Please, know that I would never harm you intentionally.

I am somewhat satisfied. The death of my father and sister is motivation for revenge, but I am an honorable man. I accept your apologies and love for what they are.

[handwritten annotations:]
his gut is right!

Horatio does not want this to happen

an apology to Laertes

none of it was on purpose

seems to forgive him

I do receive your offer'd love like love,
And will not wrong it.

HAMLET
I embrace it freely;
And will this brother's wager frankly play.
Give us the foils. Come on.

Thank you. Let's play a friendly game. Give us the weapons.

LAERTES
Come, one for me.

Give me one, too.

HAMLET
I'll be your foil, Laertes: in mine ignorance
Your skill shall, like a star i' the darkest night,
Stick fiery off indeed.

I'm going to go easy, Laertes, and make you look like a shining star in the darkest night.

LAERTES
You mock me, sir.

Don't mock me, sir.

HAMLET
No, by this hand.

I'm not.

KING CLAUDIUS
Give them the foils, young Osric. Cousin Hamlet,
You know the wager?

Give them the weapons, young Osric. Hamlet, you know what's at stake?

HAMLET
Very well, my lord
Your grace hath laid the odds o' the weaker side.

Yes, my lord. You have bet against the odds.

KING CLAUDIUS
I do not fear it; I have seen you both:
But since he is better'd, we have therefore odds.

I'm not afraid. I have seen you both, but since he's better we've given him a handicap.

LAERTES
This is too heavy, let me see another.

This sword is too heavy. Let me see another.

HAMLET
This likes me well. These foils have all a length?
They prepare to play

This one fits me well. Are they all the same length?

OSRIC
Ay, my good lord.

Yes, my lord.

KING CLAUDIUS
Set me the stoops of wine upon that table.
If Hamlet give the first or second hit,
Or quit in answer of the third exchange,
Let all the battlements their ordnance fire:
The king shall drink to Hamlet's better breath;
And in the cup an union shall he throw,
Richer than that which four successive kings
In Denmark's crown have worn. Give me the cups;
And let the kettle to the trumpet speak,
The trumpet to the cannoneer without,
The cannons to the heavens, the heavens to earth,
'Now the king dunks to Hamlet.' Come, begin:
And you, the judges, bear a wary eye.

Put the wine on that table. If Hamlet begins to win, I'll drink to his health. Then, I will put a poison in the cup stronger than the last four kings of Denmark combined. Give me the cups. Let the drum and trumpeters begin. Let's begin. Watch, judges.

HAMLET
Come on, sir.

Come on, sir.

[handwritten: wants it to be friendly]

[handwritten: Hamlet is confident]

[handwritten: this is a lie claudius wants Laertes to win]

LAERTES
Come, my lord.
They play

Come, my lord.

HAMLET
One.

One.

LAERTES
No.

No.

HAMLET
Judgment.

Judges?

OSRIC
A hit, a very palpable hit.

It was a hit.

LAERTES
Well; again.

Well, try that again.

Hamlet won the round (handwritten)

KING CLAUDIUS
Stay; give me drink. Hamlet, this pearl is thine;
Here's to thy health.

Someone give me a drink. Hamlet, this pearl is for you, and here's to your health.

Trumpets sound, and cannon shot off within

Give him the cup.

Give him the cup.

HAMLET
I'll play this bout first; set it by awhile. Come.

I don't want it right now. Just, set it down. Come on.

They play

Another hit; what say you?

Is the cup poisoned? (handwritten)

I think that was another hit. And, you?

LAERTES
A touch, a touch, I do confess.

You did touch me, I confess.

KING CLAUDIUS
Our son shall win.

Our son is going to win.

QUEEN GERTRUDE
He's fat, and scant of breath.
Here, Hamlet, take my napkin, rub thy brows;
The queen carouses to thy fortune, Hamlet.

He's fat and out of breath. Here, Hamlet, take my napkin and rub the sweat out of your eyes. I drink to your future, Hamlet.

HAMLET
Good madam!

that seems very nice (handwritten)

Thank you, madam!

KING CLAUDIUS
Gertrude, do not drink.

Gertrude, do not drink from that cup.

QUEEN GERTRUDE
I will, my lord; I pray you, pardon me.

I will, my lord. Now, if you'll excuse me.

KING CLAUDIUS
[Aside]
It is the poison'd cup: it is too late.

I was right! (handwritten)

It's the poisoned cup. It's too late.

HAMLET
I dare not drink yet, madam; by and by.

I don't want anything to drink, yet. Maybe, later.

QUEEN GERTRUDE
Come, let me wipe thy face.

Come, let my wipe your face.

LAERTES
My lord, I'll hit him now.

My lord, I'll hit him now.

KING CLAUDIUS
I do not think't.

I don't think so.

LAERTES
[Aside]
And yet 'tis almost 'gainst my conscience.

I almost feel wrong about this.

HAMLET
Come, for the third, Laertes: you but dally;
I pray you, pass with your best violence;
I am afeard you make a wanton of me.

Have you come for the third, Laertes. You are too late. Take your best shot. I'm not a child; I'm ready.

he feels Sort of bad about this

LAERTES
Say you so? come on.

Oh yea? Come on.

They play

OSRIC
Nothing, neither way.

They are so close.

LAERTES
Have at you now!

Here's one for you.

LAERTES wounds HAMLET; then in scuffling, they change rapiers, and HAMLET wounds LAERTES

KING CLAUDIUS
Part them; they are incensed.

Pull them apart. They aren't playing.

they have gotten violent

HAMLET
Nay, come, again.

No, let us go again.

QUEEN GERTRUDE falls

OSRIC
Look to the queen there, ho!

Someone look after the queen!

HORATIO
They bleed on both sides. How is it, my lord?

They are both bleeding. How are you, my lord?

OSRIC
How is't, Laertes?

How are you, Laertes?

So much is happening

LAERTES
Why, as a woodcock to mine own springe, Osric;
I am justly kill'd with mine own treachery.

Like a trapped animal, Osric. I am killed by my own evil desires.

HAMLET
How does the queen?

How's the queen?

KING CLAUDIUS
She swounds to see them bleed.

She just fainted at the sight of the blood.

QUEEN GERTRUDE
No, no, the drink, the drink,--O my dear Hamlet,--

No, no, it's the drink. Oh, my dear Hamlet,

↳ she knows of the poison

The drink, the drink! I am poison'd.

the drink is poisoned. I am dying.

Dies
HAMLET
O villany! Ho! let the door be lock'd:
Treachery! Seek it out.

Oh, what villains! Lock the door. Find out who did this.

LAERTES
It is here, Hamlet: Hamlet, thou art slain;
No medicine in the world can do thee good;
In thee there is not half an hour of life;
The treacherous instrument is in thy hand,
Unbated and envenom'd: the foul practise
Hath turn'd itself on me lo, here I lie,
Never to rise again: thy mother's poison'd:
I can no more: the king, the king's to blame.

It is likely is the king

Here, Hamlet. You are as good as dead. Nothing can save you now. You have less than an hour. The sword's tip was poisoned. Your mother is poisoned, and it's the king's fault.

HAMLET
The point!--envenom'd too!
Then, venom, to thy work.

finally tells him

The sword is poisoned. Then, let the venom do its work!

Stabs KING CLAUDIUS

All
Treason! treason!

Treason! Treason!

KING CLAUDIUS
O, yet defend me, friends; I am but hurt.

I am only hurt. Defend me, friends.

HAMLET
Here, thou incestuous, murderous, damned Dane,
Drink off this potion. Is thy union here?
Follow my mother.

*Here you incestuous, murderous, Dane.
Damn you to hell. Drink the rest of this, and go with my mother.*

KING CLAUDIUS dies

LAERTES
He is justly served;
It is a poison temper'd by himself.
Exchange forgiveness with me, noble Hamlet:
Mine and my father's death come not upon thee,
Nor thine on me.

he finally got his revenge

He got what he deserved. He poisoned himself. Please forgive me, Hamlet, and I will forgive you. My father's death or mine are not your fault, just like your death is not my fault.

Dies

HAMLET
Heaven make thee free of it! I follow thee.
I am dead, Horatio. Wretched queen, adieu!
You that look pale and tremble at this chance,
That are but mutes or audience to this act,
Had I but time--as this fell sergeant, death,
Is strict in his arrest--O, I could tell you--
But let it be. Horatio, I am dead;
Thou livest; report me and my cause aright
To the unsatisfied.

God will free you in heaven. I am on my way. I am dying, Horatio! Goodbye, wretched queen. If I had time, I could tell you all a thing or two, but death waits for no man. Horatio, tell them everything and set this story straight.

HORATIO
Never believe it:
I am more an antique Roman than a Dane:
Here's yet some liquor left.

Hamlet knows his own downfall

No one will believe it. I am more like an ancient Roman, than a corrupt Dane. Here's some poisonous drink.

HAMLET
As thou'rt a man,
Give me the cup: let go; by heaven, I'll have't.
O good Horatio, what a wounded name,
Things standing thus unknown, shall live behind me!
If thou didst ever hold me in thy heart
Absent thee from felicity awhile,
And in this harsh world draw thy breath in pain,
To tell my story.

Give me that cup.
Let go. I swear, I'll take it from you, Horatio.
If you ever cared about me, then don't do this. Stay and tell my story.

March afar off, and shot within

What warlike noise is this?

What is that noise?

[handwritten note: wants Horatio to live]

OSRIC
Young Fortinbras, with conquest come from Poland,
To the ambassadors of England gives
This warlike volley.

Young Fortinbras is returning from his triumph in Poland to greet the English ambassadors.

HAMLET
O, I die, Horatio;
The potent poison quite o'er-crows my spirit:
I cannot live to hear the news from England;
But I do prophesy the election lights
On Fortinbras: he has my dying voice;
So tell him, with the occurrents, more and less,
Which have solicited. The rest is silence.

Oh, I'm dying, Horatio.
The poison is strong. I will not live to hear the news from England, but do tell Fortinbras he has my support.

[handwritten note: won't know if there way a victory]

Dies

HORATIO
Now cracks a noble heart. Good night sweet prince:
And flights of angels sing thee to thy rest!
Why does the drum come hither?

Here lies a noble heart. Good night, sweet prince. May angels sing you to sleep! Why are those drums approaching?

March within

Enter FORTINBRAS, the English Ambassadors, and others

PRINCE FORTINBRAS
Where is this sight?

What is going on?

HORATIO
What is it ye would see?
If aught of woe or wonder, cease your search.

What do you think you see?
If you've come to see a tragedy, you've found it.

PRINCE FORTINBRAS
This quarry cries on havoc. O proud death,
What feast is toward in thine eternal cell,
That thou so many princes at a shot
So bloodily hast struck?

This looks like a massacre. Oh proud Death, what are you planning with so many royals dead at one time?

[handwritten note: that is very correct]

First Ambassador
The sight is dismal;
And our affairs from England come too late:
The ears are senseless that should give us hearing,
To tell him his commandment is fulfill'd,
That Rosencrantz and Guildenstern are dead:
Where should we have our thanks?

This is a horrible sight.
We are too late from England to tell the news of his wishes being fulfilled. Rosencrantz and Guildenstern are dead. Who is here to thank us?

HORATIO

[handwritten note: they died too?!?]

Not from his mouth,
Had it the ability of life to thank you:
He never gave commandment for their death.
But since, so jump upon this bloody question,
You from the Polack wars, and you from England,
Are here arrived give order that these bodies
High on a stage be placed to the view;
And let me speak to the yet unknowing world
How these things came about: so shall you hear
Of carnal, bloody, and unnatural acts,
Of accidental judgments, casual slaughters,
Of deaths put on by cunning and forced cause,
And, in this upshot, purposes mistook
Fall'n on the inventors' reads: all this can I
Truly deliver.

If he had the ability to thank you, Hamlet would. The king never gave the order. He did. But, since you are here to witness this scene, tell your men to put these bodies on display, and I will tell you what happened.

PRINCE FORTINBRAS
Let us haste to hear it,
And call the noblest to the audience.
For me, with sorrow I embrace my fortune:
I have some rights of memory in this kingdom,
Which now to claim my vantage doth invite me.

they will hear the story of Hamlet

Hurry. Let us hear it. Get all of the noblemen to hear it. It is with great sadness that I accept my good fortune, since I can now claim the throne.

HORATIO
Of that I shall have also cause to speak,
And from his mouth whose voice will draw on more;
But let this same be presently perform'd,
Even while men's minds are wild; lest more mischance
On plots and errors, happen.

I also have something to say about that from Hamlet, himself. Let's go ahead and start before any more madness begins.

PRINCE FORTINBRAS
Let four captains
Bear Hamlet, like a soldier, to the stage;
For he was likely, had he been put on,
To have proved most royally: and, for his passage,
The soldiers' music and the rites of war
Speak loudly for him.
Take up the bodies: such a sight as this
Becomes the field, but here shows much amiss.
Go, bid the soldiers shoot.

does not want any more chaos

Let four captains carry Hamlet, like a soldier, to the stage. He is the rightful heir to the throne. Let there be military honors to portray his heroism. Pick up the rest of the bodies. This looks like a battlefield. Fire your guns in honor of Hamlet.

A dead march. Exeunt, bearing off the dead bodies; after which a peal of ordnance is shot off.

fire guns in honor of Hamlet

End of Play

Made in United States
North Haven, CT
26 January 2023